EVERETT PUBLIC LIBRARY
Everett, WA 98201
APR   1996

D0131110

EVERETT PUBLIC LIBRARY
Everett, WA 98201
APR   1996

WESTWARD

WEST

The Epic Crossing

3 3056 00417 2055

WARD

of the American Landscape

Gerald Roscoe and David Larkin

Principal photography by Paul Rocheleau

THE MONACELLI PRESS
A David Larkin Book

"*The vast tract of untimbered country which lies between the waters of the Missouri, Mississippi, and the western ocean, from the mouth of the latter river to the 48 degree north latitude, may become in time equally celebrated as the sandy deserts of Africa. But from these immense prairies may arise one great advantage to the United States, viz: the restriction of our population to some certain limits, and thereby a continuation of the union. Our citizens being so prone to rambling and extending themselves, on the frontiers will through necessity be constrained to limit their extent on the west to the borders of the Missouri and the Mississippi, while they leave the prairies incapable of cultivation to the wandering and uncivilized aborigines of the country.*"

—Lt. Zebulon Pike, written in 1807,
after having led the first American expedition to the Southwest

"[It is] our manifest destiny to overspread and possess the whole of the continent which Providence has given us for the development of the great experiment of liberty and federated self-government entrusted to us."

—John O'Sullivan, editor of the New York *Morning News*, written in 1845

The Prairie in High Summer

THIS BOOK IS DEDICATED
TO KHANITHA
AND TO THE MEMORY OF GERRY

FIRST PUBLISHED IN THE UNITED STATES OF AMERICA IN 1995 BY
THE MONACELLI PRESS, INC.,
10 EAST 92ND STREET, NEW YORK, NEW YORK 10128.

COPYRIGHT © 1995 THE MONACELLI PRESS, INC.
PHOTOGRAPHS © 1995 PAUL ROCHELEAU EXCEPT AS CREDITED BELOW

ALL RIGHTS RESERVED UNDER INTERNATIONAL AND PAN-AMERICAN
COPYRIGHT CONVENTIONS. NO PART OF THIS BOOK MAY BE REPRODUCED OR
UTILIZED IN ANY FORM OR BY ANY MEANS, ELECTRONIC OR MECHANICAL,
INCLUDING PHOTOCOPYING, RECORDING, OR BY ANY INFORMATION STORAGE
RETRIEVAL SYSTEM, WITHOUT PERMISSION IN WRITING FROM THE PUBLISHER.
INQUIRIES SHOULD BE SENT TO THE MONACELLI PRESS, INC.

LIBRARY OF CONGRESS CATALOGING-IN-PUBLICATION DATA
ROSCOE, GERALD.
WESTWARD : THE EPIC CROSSING OF THE AMERICAN LANDSCAPE ; GERALD ROSCOE
AND DAVID LARKIN ; PRINCIPAL PHOTOGRAPHY BY PAUL ROCHELEAU.
P. CM.
INCLUDES BIBLIOGRAPHICAL REFERENCES.
ISBN 1-885254-09-1
1. WEST (U.S.)—DISCOVERY AND EXPLORATION. 2. WEST (U.S.)—
DISCOVERY AND EXPLORATION—SOURCES. 3. WEST (U.S.)—DESCRIPTION
AND TRAVEL. 4. WEST (U.S.)—DESCRIPTION AND TRAVEL—SOURCES.
I. LARKIN, DAVID, 1936– . II. ROCHELEAU, PAUL. III. TITLE.
F592.R59   1995
978'.02—DC20   95-21909

PRINTED AND BOUND IN ITALY

WE ARE GRATEFUL TO RAVEN MAPS & IMAGES FOR PERMISSION TO
REPRODUCE FROM THEIR TOPOGRAPHICAL MAP OF THE CONTINENTAL
UNITED STATES. THE ENTIRE MAP IS AVAILABLE FROM RAVEN MAPS & IMAGES,
P.O. BOX 850, MEDFORD, OREGON 97501-0253.

PHOTOGRAPH CREDITS
ALL NUMBERS REFER TO PAGE NUMBERS.
USED BY KIND PERMISSION OF BRUCE COLEMAN, INC.: GENE AHRENS 93, 224;
ERWIN AND PEGGY BAUER 23; MELINDA BERGE 112–13, 148–49, 164–65; JAMES BLANK
137; PETER COLE 222; PHIL DEGGINGER 50; LARRY R. DITTO 158; JOHN ELK III 84–85;
DAVID FALCONER 182; JOHN S. FLANNERY 181, 211; M. P. L. FOGDON 44; JEFF FOOTT 31,
42–43, 60, 88, 145, 166–67, 180, 198–99; LEE FOSTER 28; MICHAEL GALLAGHER 223; JOHN
ANGELL GRANT 175; KEITH GUNNAR 60, 229; JOHN HYDE 12–13; C. C. LOCKWOOD
61, 63, 110–11, 202, 220, 226; JOE McDONALD 82; MARK NEWMAN 152; TIMOTHY
O'KEEFE 83; LEE RENTZ 9, 104, 174; JOHN SHAW 136, 140; STEVE SOLUM 208–9;
JOHN E. SWEDBERG 48; BRUCE TUCKER 192; GARY WITNEY 6–7, 21, 135;
J. WRIGHT 4–5; BRUCE COLEMAN INC. 32–33, 74–75, 81, 160–61, 234
ARTWORK © TIG PRODUCTIONS, INC., W. BEN GLASS, PHOTOGRAPHER: 18–19, 34, 70–71
MICHAEL FREEMAN, PHOTOGRAPHER: 22, 38, 78, 175, 190

TABLE OF CONTENTS

Introduction

In 1803, when the era of the westward exploration began, just fifteen years after the establishment of the first central government of the United States, all the lands west of the Mississippi were the domain of foreign powers. And almost all were wilderness.

The Spanish had settled Santa Fe and had established isolated missions in California. The British, represented by the Hudson's Bay Company and the North West Company, had come into what the Indians called "Ouragan" to trade for beaver, as valuable as gold. The Russians remained in settlements near the coast north of today's San Francisco to hunt the furs of marine animals in the Pacific. None of these foreign powers ventured far beyond their bases with a view toward exploration or colonization.

In 1803, Napoleon, forced to concede that his dreams of a western empire had collapsed, sold the vast territory, named Louisiana in honor of the French monarch, to the young American nation. Suddenly, this country, which had not yet settled much beyond the Alleghenies, found itself more than doubled in size and in possession of a huge *terra incognita*, ready to be explored.

Beyond the Louisiana Territory, to the northwest, lay Oregon Country, which included today's Washington, Oregon, and those portions of Montana and Idaho lying west of the Continental Divide. To the southwest lay the lands of New Spain, which included today's California, Nevada, Utah, Arizona, New Mexico, Texas, western Wyoming, and western Colorado.

Few, if any, areas of the globe were as unknown and uncharted. Africa was no more mysterious than the western plains; the rain forests of South America were no more impenetrable than the mountain wildernesses; the Great Deserts of Western Australia were no more unfamiliar than America's Great Basin.

This was the land of the Indian, the land of bear and buffalo, bighorn sheep and wolves, mustangs and mountain lions, passenger pigeons that filled the skies in sun-blocking swarms. And beaver that abounded in the western streams.

Government explorers, Army explorers, fur trappers, mountain men, missionaries, emigrants, young soldiers, and pioneer settlers saw this West. In a few short decades they blazed the trails that opened it. They found elusive passes over the mountains, water holes on the arid plains, viable routes through the deserts. They were the pathfinders of the Oregon Trail, the Santa Fe Trail, the California Trail. They located the best sites for trading posts, military forts, towns and cities, railroad lines. They discovered the ruins of ancient cliff-dwellers, the wonders of Yellowstone, Yosemite, the Grand Canyon, Petrified Forest, Grand Teton, and Canyonlands.

And they described to the world what they had seen, what they had done and what they had found—in journals and diaries, in reports to Congress and to the U.S. Army, in letters to relatives and friends, in reminiscences and autobiographies. From these sources, and from present-day photographs, comes our view of the West as it was, in its vastness, unknown, seen for the first time by those who would make it their own.

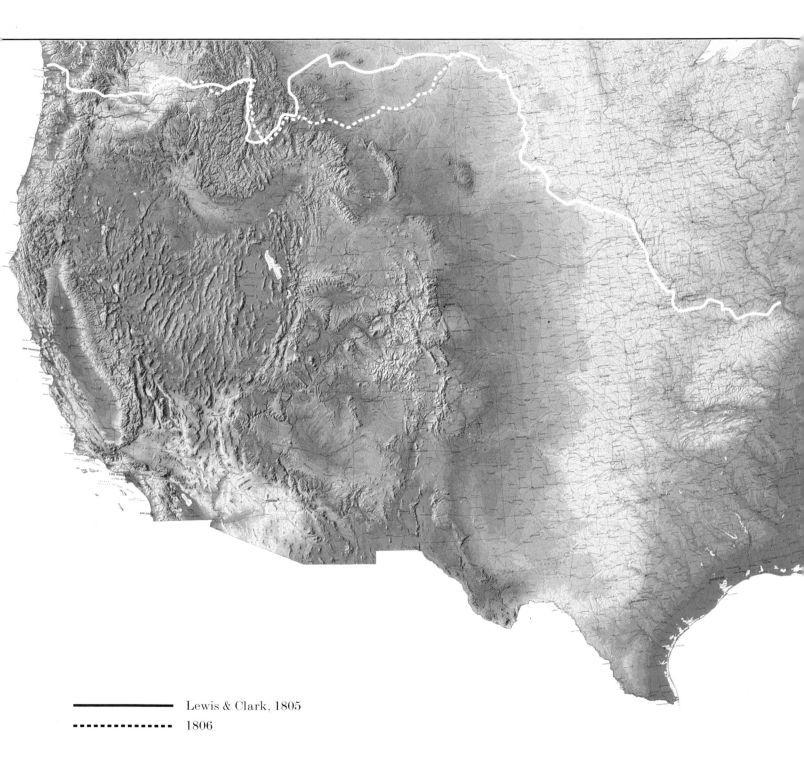

———————— Lewis & Clark, 1805

▬ ▬ ▬ ▬ ▬ ▬ ▬ 1806

Meriwether Lewis and William Clark kept daily journals, as did two other members of the party, Sergeant John Ordway and Sergeant Patrick Gass. These formed the basis of the first History *of the expedition, published in 1814, written by Nicholas Biddle, and later edited, in 1893, by Elliott Coues. The narrative that follows is based on the Bidwell-Coues edition, with direct quotes extracted from* Original Journals of the Lewis and Clark Expedition, *edited by Reuben Thwaites, 1904.*

Chapter 1

LEWIS AND CLARK: THE OPENING OF THE NORTHWEST

The Meriwether Lewis and William Clark Expedition was the curtain-raiser, the first expedition to enter the western wilderness, ascend the Missouri River, cross the Rocky Mountains, find the Columbia River and reach the Pacific Ocean.

It was the official government expedition dispatched by President Thomas Jefferson, in 1804, to explore the northwest section of the nation's newly-acquired and totally uncharted Louisiana Territory to determine if there was a river route all the way to the Pacific, to ascertain if there might be a worthwhile potential for commerce, and to establish a precedent for the United States to claim the territory to the west of the Louisiana Purchase.

The twenty-nine-man Corps of Discovery departed on May 14, 1804, from a camp located at the junctions of the Wood (DuBois), Mississippi, and Missouri rivers, in a keelboat built for navigating the tricky waters of the Missouri. The boat was fifty-five feet long, with one sail and twenty-two oars. For the first leg of the trip, the party was accompanied by two pirogues, one of which was manned by soldiers, the other by rivermen.

The Missouri was a difficult river to navigate, with rapid currents, falling banks, and shifting sand bars. The weather was oppressively hot, frequently stormy, and at times the boat had to be towed by handlines from the shore. Mosquitoes and ticks were exceedingly troublesome. But the expedition made steady headway, and by late June arrived at the mouth of the Kansas River (site of today's Kansas City, Missouri). On the banks of the river were two Indian villages, its members "now hunting on the plains for buffalo, which our hunters have seen for the first time."

In late July, as the river ascended what is now the Nebraska-Iowa border, the party reached the mouth of the Platte River. Sergeant Floyd was here "seized with a bilious colic, and all

Photograph by W. Ben Glass

our care and attention were ineffectual to relieve him. He was buried on the top of the bluff with the honors due to a brave soldier. About a mile beyond this place, to which we gave his name [Floyd's Bluff, near today's Sioux City, Iowa], is a small river which we called Floyd's River." Floyd would be the expedition's only fatality.

After three months of travel without overt hostility, the party had a number of encounters with the powerful Sioux Indians. At the site of today's Pierre, South Dakota, the expected crisis occurred. The travelers stood firm, prepared to fight in order to continue their journey, and the Sioux relented.

Lewis and Clark did not at the time realize what beneficial consequences their resolute behavior toward the Sioux would produce. Word quickly spread among the Indian tribes up the Missouri and beyond, that the Americans could not be bullied, intimidated, or stopped.

At the end of October, the party reached the Mandan villages (near today's Bismarck, North Dakota), where the captains decided to make camp and spend the winter awaiting resumption of the voyage. It was a timely decision, for as they built their post, which they named Fort Mandan, the river began to fill with ice.

Among the Mandans' neighbors, the Minnetarees, was a man named Toussaint Charbonneau, a trader. He asked Lewis and Clark to hire him as an interpreter, and they did, thereby acquiring one of the party's greatest future assets, Charbonneau's young Shoshone wife, Sacajawea, then in the late stages of pregnancy. Captain Lewis noted her delivery of a "fine boy" on February 11.

Charbonneau would be occasionally troublesome and frequently inept on the journey westward. Sacajawea would be helpful and admirable in every way, and at a crucial point

FORT MANDAN, NORTH DAKOTA

in the mountains, indispensable. The baby boy, who made the entire trip with the expedition, became a special favorite of the men.

On April 7, 1805, the expedition departed from the Mandan villages to resume the river voyage and "to penetrate a country at least 2000 miles in width on which the foot of civilized man had never trodden." The party proceeded through what is today North Dakota, in six small canoes and two large pirogues, enjoying good hunting in the midst of "immense quantities of buffalo, elk, deer, antelopes, geese, and some swans and ducks." Captain Lewis observed that "the buffalo, elk and antelope are so gentle that we pass near them while feeding without appearing to excite any alarm among them."

CONFLUENCE OF THE MISSOURI AND YELLOWSTONE RIVERS

At the mouth of the river "which had been known to the French as the Roche Jaune," and which Lewis and Clark were the first to translate as "Yellowstone," the party saw its first two grizzly bears, a species previously unknown. The captains called them "white bears," and noted that the Indians had "given us dreadful accounts of their strength and ferocity." Lewis and a hunter brought down one of the grizzlies and observed that the 300-pound beast was a "furious animal and very remarkable for the wounds which it will bear without dying."

Near the end of May, the party sighted the mountains ahead, the Little Rockies of northern Montana. Like all subsequent travelers to the West, Lewis found the snow-clad summits thrilling and climactic: "I felt a secret pleasure in finding myself so near the head of the heretofore conceived boundless Missouri, but when I reflected on the difficulties which this snowy barrier would most probably throw in my way to the Pacific, and the sufferings and hardships of myself and party in them, it in some measure counterbalanced the joy I had felt in the first moments in which I gazed on them."

THE FOOTHILLS OF THE ROCKIES IN MAY

At the Judith River, which Clark named in honor of the young woman whom he would later marry, the party came across the site of an unusual Indian buffalo hunt, which Lewis described: "We passed a precipice about 120 feet high, under which lay scattered the fragments of at least 100 carcasses of buffaloes, although the water which had washed away the lower part of the hill must have carried off many of the dead. These buffaloes had been chased down the precipice in a way very common on the Missouri, by which vast herds are destroyed in a moment.

"The mode of hunting is to select one of the most active and fleet young men, who is disguised by a buffalo-skin round his body; the skin of the head with the ears and horns being fastened on his own head in such a way as to deceive the buffalo. Thus dressed he fixes himself at a convenient distance between a herd of buffalo and any of the river precipices, which sometimes extend for some miles. His companions in the meantime get in the rear and side of the herd, and at a given signal show themselves and advance toward the buffaloes.

"These instantly take the alarm, and finding the hunters beside them, they run toward the disguised Indian, who leads them at full speed toward the river; when, suddenly securing himself in some crevice of the cliff which he had previously fixed on, the herd is left on the brink of the precipice. It is then in vain for the foremost buffaloes to retreat or even to stop; they are pressed on by the hindmost rank, which, seeing no danger but from the hunters, goad on those before them till the whole are precipitated, and the shore is strewn with their dead bodies.

"Sometimes, in this perilous seduction, the Indian is himself either trodden under foot by the rapid movements of the buffaloes, or missing his footing in the cliff is urged down the precipice by the falling herd. The Indians then select as much meat as they wish; the rest is abandoned to the wolves, and creates a most dreadful stench."

Early in June of 1805, the expedition came to the junction of a large river flowing from the north, and the captains were faced with a serious dilemma. Was this the Missouri itself forking northward or a branch which the Minnetarees at Fort Mandan had called "the river that scolds at all others"? Which one should they follow?

The expedition was divided into two parties, with Captain Clark leading one to scout the south fork, Captain Lewis leading the other to scout the north. After the scouting parties returned, "it was agreed that [while the rest of the expedition waited, Lewis and a party] should ascend the southern branch by land until they reached either the falls or the mountains." Were they to reach the falls, they would know that they were on the right course, for the Minnetarees had told the captains to be on the alert for the Great Falls of the Missouri.

After Lewis had ascended the river a few days, "his ears were saluted with the agreeable sound of a fall of water, and, as he advanced, a spray arose above the plain like a column of smoke and vanished in an instant. Toward this point he directed his steps; the noise increased as he approached, and soon became too tremendous to be mistaken for anything but the Great Falls of the Missouri. Seating himself on some rocks under the center of the falls, he enjoyed the sublime spectacle of this stupendous object, which since the creation has been lavishing its magnificence upon the desert, unknown to civilization."

But now, to proceed along the Missouri would require circumventing the Great Falls. The men built crude truck beds with wooden wheels, coupling tongs and bodies in order to haul the boats and equipment. They "put on double soles to protect them, in rain, from the prickly pear cactus, and from the sharp points of earth which have been formed by the trampling of the buffalo during the late rains. This of itself is sufficient to render the portage disagreeable to one who has no burden, but as the men are loaded as heavily as their strength will permit, the crossing is really painful. At almost every stopping place [the men] fall, and many of them are asleep in an instant; yet no one complains, and they go on with great cheerfulness."

After the eighteen-mile portage of the Falls (now submerged by the waters of a power plant), the boats were again launched, and as the party entered the Missouri Canyon with its swift currents and bordering cliffs, the river "now became much more crooked. Nothing can be imagined more tremendous than the frowning darkness [of the overhanging cliffs] which project over the river and menace us with destruction. This extraordinary range of rocks [at today's Helena, Montana] we called the Gates of the Rocky Mountains."

WILDFLOWERS IN MONTANA

Beyond the canyon lay "a beautiful plain, ten or twelve miles wide extending as far as the eye could reach. We were delighted to find that the Indian woman recognizes the country."

At the Three Forks, where three converging mountain streams give birth to the Missouri River, Lewis and Clark named them the Jefferson, the Madison, and the Gallatin. The ascent of the Missouri had come to an end, and the next leg of the journey would have to be made overland. "With no information of the route we may be unable to find a passage across the mountains, at least such a pass as will lead us to the Columbia. Even are we so fortunate as to find a branch of that river, the timber we have hitherto seen in the mountains does not promise any fit to make canoes, so that our chief dependence is on meeting some tribe from whom we may procure horses."

The long trek was now taking its toll, and some of the men were falling ill. Charbonneau suffered from a bad ankle, Captain Lewis from dysentery and fatigue, Captain Clark with a painful tumor on his ankle.

With Clark temporarily disabled and requiring rest, Lewis went ahead with a party of three, determined to find the Shoshones. At Sacajawea's suggestion, they headed across a high plain, along the Beaver Head (near today's Dillon, Montana). They crossed the Continental Divide at Lemhi Pass, the first Americans to travel beyond the Louisiana Territory into Oregon Country.

The Shoshones agreed to escort Lewis to the Indian camp where he would try to trade for the horses without which the expedition would have ended in failure. They took Lewis to the shore of a stream, the Lemhi River, and informed him that it led to the Salmon River, which would take the expedition to the Columbia. But the Lemhi, he said, was not navigable.

When Clark and Lewis were reunited, they met with the Shoshone chief, Cameahwait, whom Sacajawea recognized to be her brother. Cameahwait, who had previously been reluctant to give up any of his tribe's horses, now agreed to do so. During the few days required to round up horses, Clark determined that the Lemhi river was not navigable, and the party had no choice but to proceed on horseback.

An elderly Shoshone named Toby, and his son, agreed to serve as guides, and the party moved northward to the valley of the Bitterroot River. Near today's Missoula, the expedition turned westward into the mountains to find the mountain pass. The trail was difficult, "hills high and rocky on each side, so steep that several horses slipped and injured themselves very much." There was snow on the ground, rain fell, then sleet. The men persevered, encamping briefly on the banks of Lolo Creek at a spot they called Travellers Rest. (Today U.S. Highway 12 crosses the Bitterroot Mountains roughly along the trail on Lolo Pass taken by the expedition, and is called, in Idaho, the Lewis and Clark Highway.)

After seven arduous days in the mountains, Clark and a few men left the main party in search of a way out, and found it, coming upon a band of Nez Perce Indians. Lewis and the others caught up with them, and the Nez Perce prepared a meal of "buffalo meat, some dried salmon, berries, and several kinds of roots" for the entire party. The Nez Perce, admired by Lewis and Clark and by all subsequent travelers, informed the party that a river called the Koskooskee (today's Clearwater) lay ahead, that it was navigable, and that it led to the Snake River (at a point where today's Lewiston, Idaho, lies on the east bank, and Clarkston, Washington, on the west).

Most members of the party were now suffering severely from dysentery, but those who were able built canoes for the descent of the Clearwater. The party embarked, negotiated a series

Beacon Rock on the Columbia River

of turbulent rapids, lost one boat, which capsized on the rocks without any casualties, and reached the confluence of the Snake River.

After six days on the Snake, losing another canoe to the rapids, but again with no casualties, the expedition arrived at the Columbia River (near today's Pasco, Washington, at what is now the Sacajawea State Park), where "The multitudes of [salmon] are almost inconceivable. The water is so clear that they can readily be seen at the depth of 15 or 20 feet."

The party came to the rapids of the Short Narrows of the Dalles (now covered by the waters of Bonneville Dam), "and with great care were able to get through, to the astonishment of all the Indians, who had collected to see us from the top of the rocks." Next came the Long Narrows, another hazardous three-mile stretch, and again a crowd of Indians watched from the cliffs above, waiting in vain to salvage what might be lost should any of the canoes capsize.

Large numbers of sea otters, the basis of the Northwest coastal trade, were seen in the river, and the men knew that they were nearing the Pacific Ocean. At today's Pillar Rock, Clark noted, "Great joy in camp, we are in view of the Ocean, this great Pacific Ocean which we have been so long anxious to see, and the roaring or noise made by the waves breaking on the rocky shores, as I suppose, may be heard distinctly." (He was mistaken, however; the party was too far from the ocean to see it from Pillar Rock.)

After strong gales stalled the party (at Gray's Bay) for several days, the wind stopped and the party "instantly loaded the canoes and left the miserable spot to which we have been confined."

Photograph taken on November 18, 1992, exactly 187 years after Clark first saw the Pacific Ocean from this spot

The next morning was "clear and beautiful; our camp is in full view of the ocean." Captain Lewis led a party to Cape Disappointment at the mouth of the river "and the sea coast to the north for some distance." After examining the coast "it became necessary to decide on the spot for our wintering quarters." The captains selected a site away from the coast on what they called the Netul River, now the Lewis and Clark River, "in a thick grove of lofty pines." Clark noted that he was happy to leave the coast: "The sea roars like a repeated rolling thunder and has roared in that way ever since our arrival on its borders. I can't say Pacific, as since I have seen it, it has been the reverse." But before leaving the coast, he carved on a pine tree overlooking the ocean, words which were to become famous: "William Clark December 3rd 1805. By Land from the U. States in 1804 & 1805."

The expedition had been a brilliant success. Three months after its return, Jefferson in his annual message to Congress, said: "The expedition of Messrs. Lewis and Clark, for exploring the river Missouri, and the best communication from that to the Pacific Ocean, has had all the success which could have been expected. They have traced the Missouri nearly to its source, descended the Columbia to the Pacific Ocean, ascertained with accuracy the geography of that interesting communication across our continent, learned the character of the country, its commerce, and inhabitants; it is but justice to say that Messrs. Lewis and Clark, and their brave companions, have by this arduous service deserved well of their country."

SIGNATURE ROCK WHERE CLARK CARVED HIS NAME ON THE RETURN JOURNEY

Pike's account of his experiences was published in 1810, entitled An Account of Expeditions to the Sources of the Mississippi, and Through the Western Part of Louisiana, to the Sources of the Arkansas, Kans, Laplatte, and Pierre Jaun Rivers. *The account was disorderly and confusing, possibly because some of Pike's journals had been confiscated by the Spanish, thus forcing him to rely on memory. In 1895, Elliott Coues, noted authority on Western exploration, produced a book that stood as the authoritative reference until 1966, when* The Journals of Zebulon Montgomery Pike *was published by preeminent scholar and historian Donald Jackson. This work, along with the Coues edition and other sources, were the basis for the intriguing story of America's second epic exploration in the West.*

Chapter 2

ZEBULON PIKE: THE OPENING OF THE SOUTHWEST

Somewhere in the Southwest lay the borderline between America's recently acquired Louisiana Territory and lands long possessed by imperial Spain, but that borderline had not been clearly defined by the Louisiana Purchase. Neither had it been explored or charted, and whatever maps existed were based largely on conjecture. The United States claimed that the vast territory ceded by Napoleon extended to the Red River in the Southwest (north of the Spanish province of Texas); to the Arkansas River as far as the Rocky Mountains; and northward along the Continental Divide to Canada.

Lewis and Clark had gone beyond the Continental Divide in the Northwest into Oregon Country, although this extraterritorial excursion had not been condoned by foreign powers. When the United States planned its first exploration into the Southwest, however, there was considerable Spanish concern. Spain felt America's threat to its territories, and also claimed the Louisiana Territory borderline lay far to the east of the border defined by the United States. In addition, the land was already inhabited by Indians.

Under these conditions, in July 1806, an expedition to the Southwest was dispatched by the commander of the United States Army and governor of the Louisiana Territory, General James Wilkinson. Leadership of the expedition was entrusted to a twenty-seven-year-old career soldier, the general's protégé, Lieutenant Zebulon Montgomery Pike.

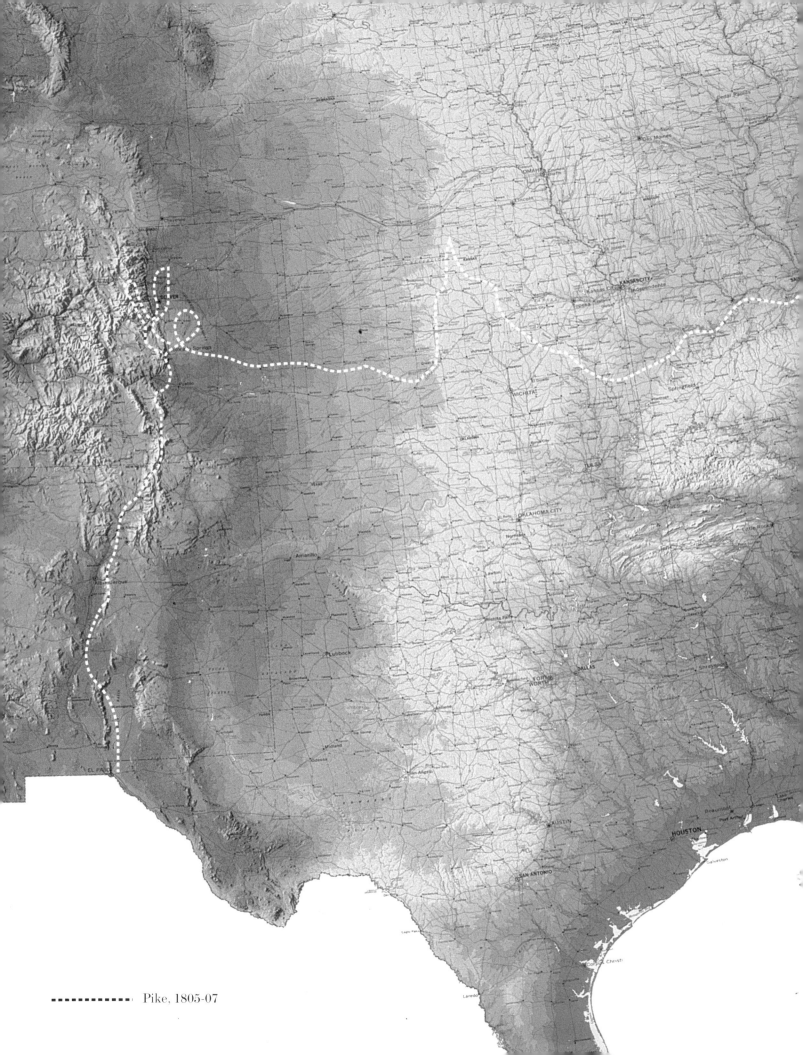

Pike, 1805-07

Lieutenant Pike was given two sets of instructions, one official, the other unofficial. Officially, Pike was assigned to effect peace treaties between and among the inhabiting Indian tribes and the Americans and to "remark particularly upon the geographical structure, the natural history, and the population of the country through which you may pass; to ascertain the direction, extent and navigation of the Arkansas and the Red River" (the presumed borders of the Louisiana Territory). Pike was cautioned, officially, that at the headwaters of the Arkansas and the Red, he would find himself "approximate to the settlements of New Mexico, and therefore it will be necessary you should move with great circumspection" to avoid giving offense to the Spanish.

Unofficially, Pike was told that his was a spy mission, that he was expected to ascertain the numbers, strength, military readiness, and locations of the Spanish forces within and to the west of the southern reaches of the Louisiana Territory.

Pike's party embarked "from the landing at Belle Fontaine" (a few miles above St. Louis) on the Missouri River. It included a large group of Osage Indians to be escorted to their towns. On August 15, the Indians were reunited with their tribe at the Osage village (near Osceola, Missouri).

When the Osage chiefs gathered for council with Pike, he told them that he had been ordered "to bring the Osages and Kans together, to smoke the pipe of peace, to bury the tomahawk, and to become as one nation." Four Osage chiefs agreed to accompany Pike to the Pawnee Republic where they would meet the Kan.

After spending about three weeks among the Osages, and securing horses from them to make the rest of his journey overland, Pike turned away from the river and headed west, to begin the first official American expedition into the unknown land of today's Kansas and beyond.

THE PRAIRIE IN EARLY SEPTEMBER

"The prairies," he noted, "rising and falling in regular swells, as far as the sight can extend, produce a very beautiful appearance." The early September weather was generally hot and dry, and the men occasionally "suffered much with drought." But game was plentiful. As Pike wrote, he "stood on a hill and in one view below me saw buffalo, elk, deer, cabrie [antelopes], and panthers." He allowed the hunters to kill what they needed for sustenance, but prevented the men from shooting indiscriminately at the game, "not merely because of the scarcity of ammunition, but, as I conceived, the laws of morality forbid it also."

THE ARKANSAS RIVER

The party followed the Kansas River "over a series of hills and hollows," and on a day of heavy rain rested from what had been many days of long and exhausting marches. "We employed ourselves in reading the Bible, Pope's Essays, and in pricking on our arms with India ink some characters which will frequently bring to mind our forlorn and dreary situation, as well as the happiest days of our life."

On the way to the Pawnee villages, Pike met an Indian hunter who told him that a "party of 300 Spaniards had lately been seen" somewhere in the area. A few days later the party "struck a very large road on which the Spanish troops returned and on which we could yet discover the grass beaten down in the direction which they went." When Pike arrived at the Pawnee village (on the Republican River just inside today's Nebraska state line) the chief,

known as Caracterish, or White Wolf, confirmed that Spanish troops had visited his tribe. This was a startling bit of news, for the Pawnees were far to the east of the defined Spanish territories.

What Pike did not know, and never did learn, was that his expedition had been reported to the Spanish by the very man who had dispatched it, General James Wilkinson. The commander of the United States Army, documents have since revealed, was a secret agent of the Spanish.

President Thomas Jefferson, meanwhile, knew nothing of Wilkinson's intrigues; Wilkinson had dispatched the Pike expedition without the knowledge or consent of the President of the United States, confident that there would be no objections to it.

Wilkinson was, presumably, sending Pike on a Red River survey, and it is quite possible that Pike actually intended to search for the source of the river, for that is where he had the best chances of meeting the Comanche Indians. That he wound up on the Rio Grande River instead, pretending that he thought it to be the Red, was part of his secret espionage assignment, which he, unaware of Wilkinson's private intrigues, believed to be in his country's best interests.

THE LOWER RIDGES OF PIKE'S PEAK, COLORADO

PHOTO BY W. BEN GLASS

After a stay with the Pawnees that ended in a confrontation similar to that of Lewis and Clark's episode with the Sioux, Pike and his party marched southward through Kansas, and reached the Arkansas River at its great bend. Pike's main party of fifteen continued the march westward along the Arkansas. "I will not attempt," Pike wrote, "to describe the droves of animals we saw. Suffice it to say that the face of the prairie was covered with them on each side of the river; their numbers exceeded imagination." In mid-November, inside today's Colorado state line, Pike caught his first sight of the "Mexican mountains" (Spanish Peaks). His small party "with one accord gave three cheers." The appearance of the mountains "can be easily imagined by those who have crossed the Alleghany; but their sides were whiter as if covered with snow, or a white stone. They appear to present a natural boundary between the province of Louisiana and New Mexico."

When the expedition reached the site of the future city of Pueblo, Colorado, Pike made his historic decision to climb to the summit of a mountain ahead "in order to be enabled from its pinical to lay down the various branches and positions of the country. We commenced ascending, found it very difficult, being obliged to climb up rocks, sometimes almost perpendicular; and after marching all day, we encamped in a cave, without blankets, victuals, or water."

Dawn found them "hungry, dry, and extremely sore from the unequality of the rocks on which we had lain all night, but [we] were amply compensated for toil by the sublimity of the prospects below." Pike's goal was to reach the summit of what he called Grand Peak, "entirely bare of vegetation and covered with snow." He discovered that the peak "now appeared at the distance of fifteen or sixteen miles from us, and as high again as what we had ascended, and would have taken a whole day's march to have arrived at its base, when I believe no human being could have ascended to its pinical." He gave up the attempted climb of what is now known as Pike's Peak.

Now the ordeal of the Rockies was to begin for Pike and his men. Snow started to fall, and the party was marooned for two days by a heavy blizzard. The horses "were attacked by magpies who, attracted by the scent of their sore backs, alighted on them, and in defiance of their wincing and kicking, picked many places quite raw." On the move again, "two of the men got their feet froze" fording a river. Pike's plight was made even worse by the realization that he was lost.

In his wanderings Pike came to a river (the South Platte) whose banks for "at least six miles were covered with horse dung and the marks of Indian camps, which had been since the cold weather, as was evident by the fires which were in the centre of the lodges; the sign made by their horses was astonishing, and would have taken a thousand horses some months. The geography of the country had turned out to be so different from our expectation, we were somewhat at a loss which course to pursue unless we attempted to cross the snowcapped mountains [the Sangre de Cristo Range] to the southeast of us, which was almost impossible."

On Christmas Day they were still lost in the mountains. Their situation worsened when they found themselves moving into a forbidding canyon of the Arkansas River known today as the Royal Gorge (near today's Canon City, Colorado, and spanned by one of the highest suspension bridges in the world). After a week in the Royal Gorge, the party found it "almost impossible to proceed any further with the horses by the bed of the river, ascended the mountain and immediately after were again obliged to descend an almost perpendicular side of the mountain." When they finally climbed out of the canyon, Pike realized that they were back at the site "which we had left nearly one month since! This was a great mortification. This was my birthday, and most fervently did I hope never to pass another so miserably."

SANGRE DE CRISTO MOUNTAINS

Threatened by starvation, fighting to keep alert in the freezing weather, and desperately lost, Pike and his men now faced complete disaster. It was clear that they must find a way out of the mountains or perish. The only way out would require them to tackle the apparently insurmountable Sangre de Cristo Mountains. Leaving the horses and two men behind, Pike and the others would try to cross the mountain on foot and send for the rest if they found a way out.

The march proved to be the expedition's worst ordeal. It was almost forty degrees below zero. Pike and Dr. John Robinson, who had separated from the party in order to find food, remained without any themselves for four days and "had become extremely weak and faint…We were determined to remain absent and die by ourselves rather than to return to our camp and behold the misery of our poor lads, when we discovered a gang of buffalo coming along at some distance. With great exertions I made out to run and place myself behind some cedars and by the greatest good luck, the first shot stopped one, which we killed in three more shots; and by the dusk had cut each of us a heavy load with which we determined immediately to proceed to the camp in order to relieve the anxiety of our men, and carry the poor fellows some food."

The expedition, so close to disaster, was saved. Pike found an old Indian trail and followed it past a "sand hill" which "extended up and down at the foot of the White Mountains [his name for the Sangre de Cristos] about 15 miles, and appeared to be about 5 miles in width. Their appearance was exactly that of the sea in a storm, except as to color, not the least sign of vegetation existing thereon." (The Great Sand Dunes, today a National Monument.) The mountain ordeal ended on January 30, when "we marched hard, and arrived in the evening on the banks, then supposed Red River, of the Rio Del Norte [the Rio Grande]." On the Conejos River branch of the Rio Grande (several miles south of today's Alamosa, Colorado), men set to work building a simple stockade, while a small detachment went off to "assist on the poor fellows who were left behind," and to retrieve the horses from the encampment beyond the mountains.

At the end of February, a military force of some one hundred Spaniards appeared at the Conejos stockade. Pike reports his interchange with the troop's commanding officer as follows: " 'Sir, the governor of New Mexico, being informed you had missed your route, ordered me to offer you, in his name, mules, horses, money or whatever you may stand in need of to conduct you to the head of Red River.' 'What,' said I, interrupting him, 'Is not this the Red River.' 'No sir! The Rio del Norte.' "

The commander, under instruction from the governor of New Mexico, Joaquin Alencaster, brought Pike and his men to Santa Fe to explain their "business on his frontier," giving Pike precisely the opportunity he was hoping for, a reconnoiter of the Spanish military strength.

Courteously escorted by the Spanish troops, Pike's party was taken into New Mexico on a route paralleling the Rio Grande. The party "passed several little mudwalled villages and settlements, all of which had round mud towers of the ancient shape and construction."

When the party entered "the village of St. John's [San Juan Pueblo], the house tops were crowded, as well as the streets."

From Pike's journal comes the first description by an American explorer of what is today one of the most enchanting cities in the Southwest, Santa Fe: "It is situated along the banks of a small creek, which comes down from the mountains and runs west to the Rio del Norte. The length of the capital on the creek may be estimated at one mile; it is but three streets in width. Its appearance from a distance struck my mind with the same effect as a fleet of the flat-bottomed boats which are seen in the spring and fall seasons descending the Ohio river. There are two churches, the magnificence of whose steeples form a striking contrast to the miserable appearance of the houses. On the north side of the town is the square of soldiers' houses, equal to 120 or 140 on each side. The public square is in the centre of the town, on the north side of which is situated the palace, as they term it, or government house. The streets are very narrow, say in general twenty-five feet. The supposed population is 4,500 souls."

From Santa Fe, Pike and his men were escorted to Chihuahua, then sent home to the United States by way of the Mexican province of Texas. After his return, in July 1807, Pike prepared two reports for the Army, and worked on his journals and diaries. He made extensive observations on New Spain: its population, trade and commerce, mines and minerals, religion, history, geography, government and laws, morals and manners, and of course, military capacity.

Pike's achievements were historically significant. His expedition was the first to explore some of the southwestern lands of the Louisiana Territory—across Kansas along the future Santa Fe Trail on the Arkansas River, into Colorado beyond the future site of Bent's Fort near La Junta (where the Trail would later turn southwestward to New Mexico), and over the mountains to Santa Fe. His reconnaissance of the Spanish military forces was of strategic value years later to the United States Army. His reports on New Spain attracted trappers and traders to New Mexico, and his descriptions of the routes, and his maps, guided them in their journeys.

But the first traders to enter New Mexico after Pike's return were met with suspicion and hostility by the Spanish. They were regarded as enemies and spies and were harassed and thrown into jail. Not until Mexico broke the Spanish yoke in 1821 were Americans able to move freely in Pike's footsteps. Meanwhile, however, no foreign powers stood in the way of American advances north of New Spain, and it was here that the next phase of America's westering took place.

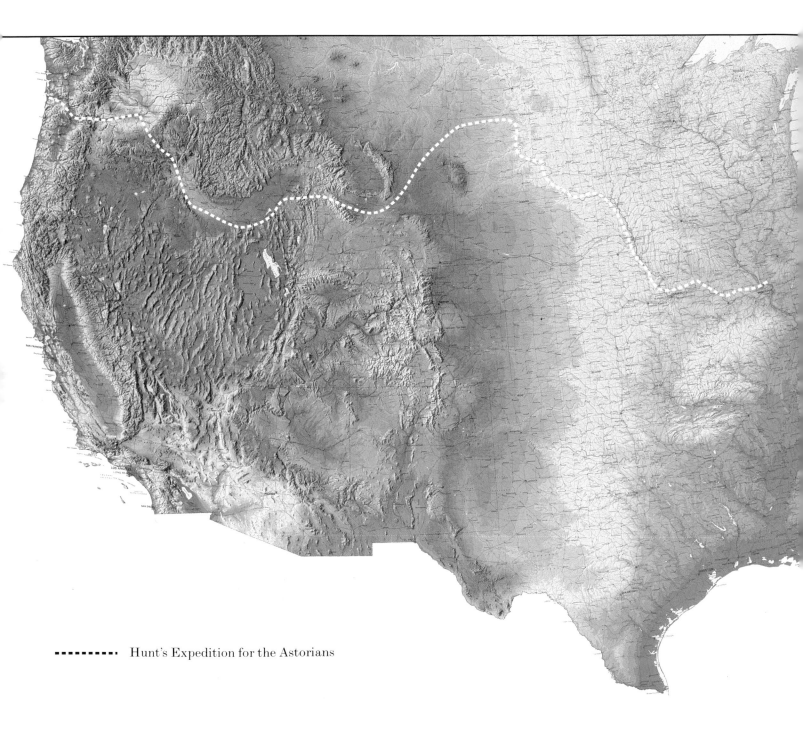

Hunt's Expedition for the Astorians

Under the management of a newly organized Missouri Fur Company, an expedition was sent up the Missouri in the summer of 1809. One of the men who joined Manuel Lisa's party, Thomas James, chronicled the events in his reminiscences Three Years Among the Indians and Mexicans. *His narrative of the Lisa expedition is the historian's sole source of information about it.*

Chapter 3

THE ASTORIANS

Manuel Lisa and The Astorians: The Fur Trappers Move Westward

While Lewis and Clark brought the American flag across the western wilderness to the Northwest Pacific, and Zebulon Pike brought it across the Southwest to New Spain, other hardy individuals were venturing into the Louisiana Territory's wilderness. They were men engaged in the fur trade, the major business of the border settlements.

The return of Lewis and Clark, with their reports of abundant beaver on the Upper Missouri, quickly changed the nature of this business. And of Western exploration.

Fur traders entered the wilderness for one purpose—to search for beaver. They did not think in terms of reconnaissance or exploration, geography or mapmaking. They did not consider themselves trailblazers, yet they blazed the major trails which, in the wake of Lewis and Clark, and Zebulon Pike, brought about the ultimate opening of the West.

Manuel Lisa, New Orleans born, of Spanish parents, was one St. Louis trader who took advantage of the Lewis and Clark report. He directed his efforts to the rich trapping grounds on the Upper Missouri which they had described.

Regarded by some as a ruthless competitor, exploiter of subordinates and insidious provocateur of Indians (whom he incited to harass his rivals), Lisa was regarded by others as a man of physical valor, intellectual acumen and resolute determination. However controversial he may have been, he played a dominant role in the exploration of this new territory.

Engaging four veterans of the Lewis and Clark journey, Lisa organized a fur-trapping expedition to ascend the Missouri and managed to establish himself as a trader with the

Sioux and the Arikaras on the lower reaches of the river. He then proceeded to the Upper Missouri and, at the confluence of the Big Horn and Yellowstone rivers, the area which Lewis and Clark had reported to be swarming with beaver, he built a post—Manuel's Fort. It was the first building erected in present-day Montana.

From this base Lisa's men fanned out through territory never before explored by Americans. One of them, John Colter, brought back descriptions of tar pits, hot springs, and geysers his fellow trappers laughed at in disbelief and dubbed "Colter's Hell." It was Yellowstone Park.

Later esteemed for this discovery and many others, as well as some remarkable feats of endurance, Colter became legendary. The mountain country of today's Wyoming was his special terrain. Not only was he first to see Yellowstone Park, but also first to explore the valley of the Bighorn River and the head of the Wind River. Colter was first to see the Grand Teton Mountains, Jackson Hole, Pierre's Hole, and the sources of the Snake River.

A second Lisa expedition was sent up the Missouri in June of 1809, and proceeded to Manuel's Fort, where Lisa left it to return to St. Louis. His trappers "were cheered with thoughts of making a speedy fortune," but they soon faced two frightening hazards: grizzly bears and Blackfeet Indians. "The men had frequent encounters with bears, which in this region are of enormous size, sometimes weighing 800 pounds each, and when wounded are the most terribly ferocious and dangerous to the hunters of all other animals."

The trappers, having come so far into the wilderness in search of their fortunes, found themselves in a nightmare. "The Blackfeet manifested so determined a hatred and jealousy

of our presence that we could entertain no hope of successfully prosecuting our business, even if we could save our lives in this country." They abandoned the fort, with most deciding to return to St. Louis. Andrew Henry, partner in the venture, was determined to bring back beaver, and led a party of men westward. They built a post, known as Henry's Fort, on the north fork of the Snake River in present-day Idaho near St. Anthony. It was the first trading post west of the Continental Divide. They lasted a winter, living on horse meat, and abandoned the post in the spring of 1811.

Manuel Lisa and his partners were not the only ones to respond to the Lewis and Clark reports. John Jacob Astor, the most powerful fur merchant of the time, enlisted Wilson Price Hunt, a former militia lieutenant from New Jersey with no wilderness experience, and Donald McKenzie, a three-hundred-pound veteran of years in the fur trade, to mount a western expedition.

Simultaneously, Lisa was organizing another expedition to ascend the Missouri from St. Louis. Outraged when he lost a man he had counted on to Hunt's rival party of fur traders, Lisa sought desperately to overtake the "Astorians." He did, and both parties continued up the Missouri in an atmosphere of suspicion and tension, each along opposite banks.

But when Lisa did not betray the Astorians in a meeting with the Arikara Indians, and remained at the Arikara village where he was later reunited with Henry, Hunt and his party made preparations to embark on the first journey to the Pacific Northwest after Lewis and Clark.

THE CANYON OF THE RIVER IN YELLOWSTONE

The details of this epic journey were narrated by Washington Irving in his classic, Astoria. *The famous American author had undertaken the work at the request of John Jacob Astor, and this work, as well as Hunt's* Diary of his Overland Trip Westward to Astoria, *are the basis of what follows.*

New Trails to the Pacific Northwest

On July 18, 1811, Wilson Price Hunt led the Astorians away from the Missouri route of Lewis and Clark and headed overland on horseback. They were to meet another group of Astorians, who had voyaged by sea to establish Fort Astoria on the Pacific Ocean at the mouth of the Columbia River in today's northwest Oregon.

"Part of their route," Washington Irving wrote of the overlanders, "would lay across an immense tract stretching north and south for hundreds of miles along the foot of the Rocky Mountains. This region, which resembles one of the immeasurable steppes of Asia, has not been inaptly termed 'the great American desert.' It spreads forth into undulating and treeless plains, and desolate sandy wastes. It is a land where no man permanently abides. The herbage is parched and withered; the brooks and streams are dried up; the buffalo, elk and deer have wandered to distant parts.

"Occasionally the monotony of this vast wilderness is interrupted by mountainous belts of sand and limestone, broken into confused masses, with precipitous cliffs and yawning ravines, looking like the ruins of a world; or is traversed by lofty and barren ridges of rock almost impassable. The rugged defiles and deep valleys form sheltering places for restless and ferocious bands of savages. We cannot be surprised, therefore, that some of the resolute of the party should feel dismay at the thoughts of adventuring into this perilous wilderness…"

THE DEVIL'S TOWER

44

THE WIND RIVER VALLEY

At the outset, however, things went well as the party rode slowly to the Big River (today's Grand) in northern South Dakota. Here they met a band of friendly Cheyenne Indians with whom they encamped until early August, hunting buffalo and laying in a supply of provisions. They purchased additional horses from the "tall, straight, and vigorous" Cheyennes, "some of whom were almost as naked as statues and might have stood as models for a statuary."

Beyond Grand River, "the country became mountainous and the water scarce." The trail was "irksome because of steepness and the great number of stones," and it led them over the Slim Buttes in today's Custer National Forest of Montana. "The country was extremely rugged, and a way out of the mountains could not be found," forcing Hunt to lead the party southwest on a long detour into the Laramie Mountains of Wyoming, known then as the Black Hills. The hills were "chiefly composed of sandstone, and in many places broken into savage cliffs and precipices, and presented the most singular and fantastic forms, sometimes resembling towns and castellated fortresses." (The party was in what is known today as Devil's Tower National Monument.)

The weather was oppressively hot. The party suffered from lack of water. One of their dogs died of fatigue. At last, in the vicinity of today's Buffalo, Wyoming, they came onto a fork of the Powder River (known then as Crazy Woman Creek), where they were able to slake their thirst, hunt for buffalo and jerk a supply of meat.

The party now found itself in Crow country at the foot of the Bighorn Mountains. "The tribe consists of four bands, which have their nestling-places in fertile, well-wooded valleys, lying among the Rocky Mountains and watered by the Big Horse River and its tributary streams…"

After crossing the Bighorns, with the help of the Crows, the Astorians "continued westward through a rugged region of hills and rocks," then to the banks of the "rapid and beautifully clear" Wind River, the north fork of the Bighorn. "For five succeeding days, Mr. Hunt and his party continued up the course of the Wind River, crossing and re-crossing it according to its windings and the nature of its banks; sometimes passing through valleys, at other times scrambling over rocks and hills."

Leaving the river, they followed an Indian trail southwesterly into the mountains, over a pass that was to become the important Union Pass. They came to a height from which they viewed one of the spectacular sights of the North American continent, the three snow-topped peaks of the Grand Tetons. They greeted the sight with great "joy at seeing the first landmarks of the Columbia," a fork of which would now not be, they thought, too far distant.

"The travellers continued their course to the south of west through a region so elevated that patches of snow lay on the highest summits and on the northern declivities. At length they came to the desired stream, the object of their search, the waters of which flowed to the west. It was, in fact, a branch of the Colorado, which falls into the Gulf of California, and had received from the hunters the name of Spanish River." This was the Green River.

"Having in the course of the last seventeen days traversed two hundred and sixty miles of rough, and in many parts sterile, mountain country, the wayworn and hungry travellers" hunted buffalo, feasted on berries, and rested for several days. Refreshed, and "now well supplied with provisions, Mr. Hunt broke up his encampment on the 24th of September, and continued on to the west. A march of fifteen miles, over a mountain ridge brought them to a stream which [John] Hoback, one of their guides, who had trapped about the neighborhood when in the service of Mr. Henry, recognized for one of the head waters of the Columbia. The travellers hailed it with delight as the first stream they had encountered tending toward their point of destination."

They followed the meanderings of the river (now known as Hoback's River), through the "stupendous defiles," into today's Jackson Hole. They then reentered the mountains, crossed them at what is now known as Teton Pass, and came to the banks of the Snake River. "They had conquered the chief difficulties of this great rocky barrier, and now flattered themselves with the hope of an easy downward course for the rest of their journey. Little did they dream of the hardships and perils by land and water which were yet to be encountered in the frightful wilderness that intervened between them and the shores of the Pacific!"

At the Snake River (which because of the tumultuous nature of its current was dubbed Mad River) Hunt was faced with deciding whether to attempt a navigation by boats or to continue overland on horseback. The men voted to proceed by boats, but Hunt was "doubtful whether [the river] might not abound with impediments lower down, sufficient to render the navigation of it slow and perilous, if not impracticable." Although he was persuaded by the men to let them start building canoes, he sent an exploring party led by John Reed, John Day, and Pierre Dorion, Jr. to scout the river ahead.

"...Two Snake Indians wandered into the camp. When they perceived that the strangers were fabricating canoes, they shook their heads and gave them to understand that the river was not navigable. Their information, however, was scoffed at by some of the party, who were obstinately bent on embarkation, but was confirmed by the exploration party, who returned after several days' absence." They had found the river to be "a narrow, crooked, turbulent stream, confined in a rocky channel, with many rapids, and occasionally overhung with precipices."

Hunt decided to abandon the Snake River and look for a more navigable stream. His men agreed, then "[Edward] Robinson, [John] Hoback, and [Jacob] Rezner, the three hunters who had hitherto served as guides among the mountains, now stepped forward and advised Mr. Hunt to make for the post established during the preceding year by Mr. Henry. They had been with Mr. Henry and, as far as they could judge by the neighboring landmarks, his post could not be very far off. Henry's post, or fort, was on an upper branch of the Columbia, down which they made no doubt it would be easy to navigate in canoes."

Guided by the two Snake Indians, the group moved northward through Pierre's Hole, now known as Teton Basin, and on Henry's Fork of the Snake River, found the deserted post. The men proceeded to construct canoes.

On October 19 the party embarked in fifteen canoes. "The current [of Henry's Fork] bore them along at a rapid rate; the light spirits of the Canadian voyageurs, which had occasionally flagged upon land, rose to their accustomed buoyancy on finding themselves again upon the water."

Entering the Snake, the character of the river abruptly changed. "The current began to foam and brawl, and assume the wild and broken character common to the streams west of the Rocky Mountains. Two of the canoes filled among the breakers; the crews were saved, but much of the lading was lost or damaged, and one of the canoes drifted down the stream and was broken among the rocks." The next day the river narrowed so abruptly and turned so violent that "they were obliged to pass the canoes down cautiously by a line from the impending banks."

The current was strong yet steady, but soon "the river again became rough and impetuous, and was chafed and broken by numerous rapids. These grew more and more dangerous, and the utmost skill was required to steer among them." They were in a roaring, rock-filled canyon, and the canoe bearing Ramsay Crooks and four others struck a rock, was split and overturned. A man was lost.

"This disastrous event brought the whole squadron to a halt, and struck a chill into every bosom." They were forced to pitch camp on the banks of the strait, which they named Caldron Linn (near today's Milner, Idaho).

After other attempts to reconnoiter the river had failed, John Reed, Robert McLellan, and Donald McKenzie went off again in various directions, while Crooks' men started back to Fort Henry to retrieve the horses. After five days, two companions of Reed's returned, and said it was impossible to proceed on the river, which was nothing but rapids and waterfalls. (In this stretch of the Snake River are located Shoshone Falls and Twin Falls, with the Shoshone, at 212 feet high, even higher than Niagara Falls.)

Crooks returned, unsuccessful, saying that it was impossible to reach Henry's Fort and return to the main body next spring. Reed and McKenzie, meanwhile, had gone off on their own, according to prior agreement that "they were to shift for themselves and shape their

Hell's Canyon, Idaho

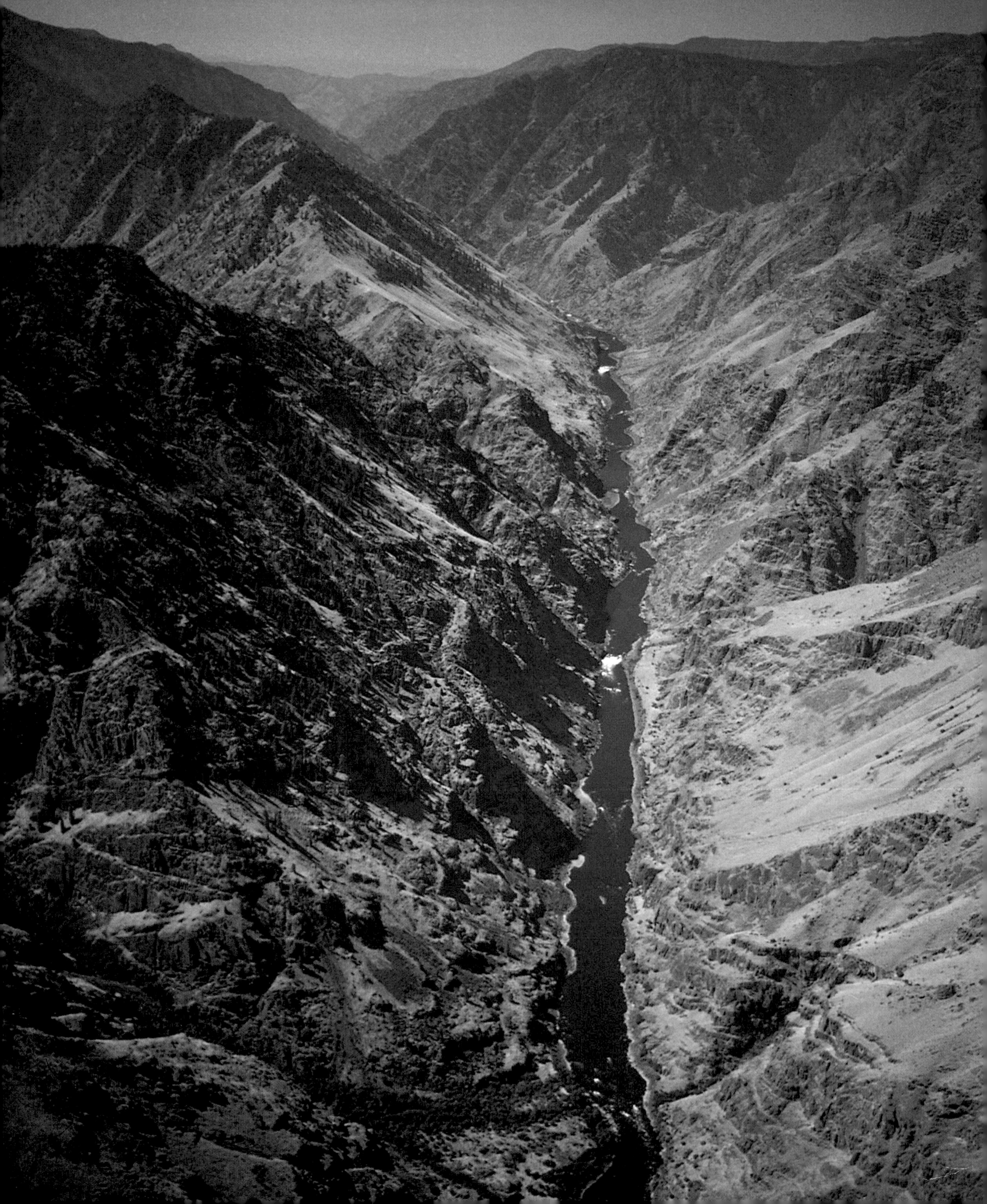

course according to circumstances." Better to split into small parties, thought Hunt, one of whom might find a way out.

Hunt and the men who remained with him now had no choice but to proceed on foot. After preparing nine caches to hide the goods that could not be carried on their backs, the men got ready to leave the scene of their disaster, unaware that they were still a thousand miles from Astoria.

"Mr. Hunt and his companions determined to keep along the course of the river," with the party divided in two "that they might have the better chance of procuring subsistence in the scanty region they were to traverse." Hunt and one group took the north side of the river; Crooks and another group, including John Day, the south.

After a few days, Hunt's men met scattered encampments of Snake Indians from whom they were able to buy dried salmon and two horses. Further arduous travel brought the party "to the banks of a beautiful little stream" (Boise River). "The weather was constantly rainy. We could not make much progress. On [November] 22nd we met some Indians. From my observations and the few words I could understand, the distance from this place to the Big River was very considerable," but they could not give Hunt any suggestions regarding which route he should follow. They continued along the Boise River and "on the 25th, despite the severe weather, our fatigue and our weakness, we forded another river [Payette River] which came from the east. The water was waist-deep."

Next, the party crossed the Weiser River and came to "a defile so narrow as to leave scarcely space enough to pass through. We frequently were obliged to remove the baggage from our horses and travel in the water. On the previous evening a beaver had been caught, which furnished us a scanty breakfast. We had supped off bouillon tablets. I therefore had a horse killed. My men found the flesh very good. I ate it reluctantly because of my fondness for the poor beast."

The trail led Hunt to "mountains so high [at the southerly end of the Seven Devils range] that I would never have believed our horses could have got over them." Snow began to fall "so densely that we could see nothing a half-mile ahead of us. The snow came above our knees. It was excessively cold. We were almost succumbing to its severity when, at sunset, we had the good fortune to reach a cluster of pines. We made a good fire, which comforted us. On [December] 5th the abundant snow which was falling did not allow us to see three hundred feet ahead of us. We succeeded, however, in reaching the [Snake] river's bank by letting ourselves slide. The sound of the running water guided us.

"On the 6th, we had just started out, when—what was my astonishment and distress!— I beheld Mr. Crooks and his party on the other side of the river." Crooks and his men were gaunt, emaciated, starving. They called across the river for food. Hunt's men constructed a flimsy canoe made with the skin of the horse they had killed. Some horse meat was paddled over to the starving men, and Crooks himself was brought back across the river. Hunt noted that Crooks, "poor man! was well-nigh spent from fatigue and want."

THE BLUE MOUNTAINS IN OREGON

After assessing the situation, Hunt announced his decision to retrace his steps. When he would not abandon the weaker party of men, Hunt's own men began to break away, until only five remained.

"On [Dec.] 16th," Hunt's journal records, "we camped on the banks of the river [the Weiser] that we had crossed on the 26th of last month. Thus, for twenty days, we had uselessly tired ourselves in seeking a route along the lower part of the [Snake] river." The only route to survival lay in crossing the Blue Mountains. The Shoshones knew of a trail and three of them were finally persuaded to guide them through. The party then returned to the Snake River where they were reunited with the remainder of Crooks' party.

On January 8, 1812, the party came out of the Blue Mountains after crossing the broad, round valley known today as the Grande Ronde and then "encountered a small stream which led us to an extremely narrow pass between immensely high mountains" (Simac Gulch). On the banks of the Umatilla River they found an encampment of Sciatoga and Tushepaw Indians. "It was with the utmost joy and most profound gratitude to heaven that Mr. Hunt found himself and his band of weary and famishing wanderers thus safely extricated from the most perilous part of their long journey, and within the prospect of a termination of their toils."

The party remained in the Indian encampment for several days. When restored to health and vigor they followed the Umatilla River on a two-day march on horseback, having bought horses from the Sciatogas. And then—"the wayworn travellers lifted up their eyes and beheld before them the long-sought waters of the Columbia."

When Hunt reached Fort Astoria, on February 15, he "had the pleasure of again meeting Messrs. McKenzie and McLellan, who had arrived more than a month before, after having suffered severe hardships." With them was John Reed.

"As the spring opened, the little settlement of Astoria was in agitation, and prepared to send forth various expeditions. Several important things were to be done." Robert Stuart, who had sailed to Astoria on the *Tonquin*, was to lead a small band carrying supplies to

THE COLUMBIA RIVER FROM THE WASHINGTON SHORE

an outpost on the Okanagan River. Russel Farnham and another small band were to find Hunt's cache at the Caldron Linn and bring the goods back to Astoria. John Reed, accompanied by Robert McLellan, was to carry despatches overland to John Jacob Astor in New York.

The three parties set off together. But after Reed was attacked and seriously wounded, and his despatches stolen, his mission was abandoned. After the parties went on to the Okanagan they turned back and retraced their steps to Astoria.

Below the forks of the Columbia, they encountered Crooks and Day, wretched and entirely naked, but alive. The overland Astorians were now reunited after their long and terrible trek from the Arikara village. Their achievement, despite confusions, blunders, and disasters, demonstrated that there were routes across the northern Rockies other than those that had been discovered by Lewis and Clark. They were the first party to see the Black Hills (Laramie Mountains) of Wyoming, first to come through the Wind River Mountains via Union Pass, first across the Tetons, first to attempt navigation of the "mad" Snake River in Idaho, and first to cross the Blue Mountains in southeastern Oregon.

The Astorians had accomplished an epic transcontinental crossing, and there was much more they would accomplish.

The Rise and Fall of Fort Astoria

The men who greeted the overland Astorians on their arrival at Fort Astoria were those who had sailed there on the eight-month voyage from New York via the Falklands, Cape Horn, and Hawaii on the *Tonquin*. Shortly after arrival the ship, with a small crew aboard, sailed again to explore coastal trade to the north.

After the arrivals at Fort Astoria of Donald McKenzie, Robert McLellan, and John Reed, in February of 1811 and, a month later, Wilson Price Hunt and his exhausted party, months were spent in preparation for sending the news of the arrival and reunion of the two expeditions.

At the end of July when rumor that "the *Tonquin* had been destroyed on the coast, and all the crew massacred by the natives," had reached Fort Astoria, "We did not give credence to this rumor." Even in December, when nothing had been heard, "We still flattered ourselves... with the hope that perhaps the vessel had sailed for the East Indies without touching at Astoria."

On May 9, the *Beaver*, dispatched by John Jacob Astor, arrived at Astoria carrying goods and reinforcements, including partner John Clarke and Ross Cox. The captain of the *Beaver* "confirmed the report of the destruction of the *Tonquin*..."

THE MOUTH AND BREAKERS OF THE COLUMBIA RIVER

Ross Cox, only eighteen when he sailed to the Northwest on the *Beaver*, describes Fort Astoria upon his arrival: "The spot selected for the fort was on a handsome eminence called Point George, which commanded an extensive view of the majestic Columbia in front, bounded by the bold and thickly-wooded northern shore. On the right, about three miles distant, a long, high, and rocky peninsula covered with timber, called Tongue Point, extended a considerable distance into the river from the southern side, with which it was connected by a narrow neck of land; while on the extreme left, Cape Disappointment, with the bar and its terrific chain of breakers was distinctly visible.

"The buildings consisted of apartments for the proprietors and clerks, with a capacious dining-hall for both, extensive warehouses for the trading goods and furs, a provision store, a trading shop, smith's forge, carpenter's workshop, etc. The whole surrounded by stockades forming a square, and reaching about fifteen feet above the ground. A gallery ran round the stockades, in which loopholes were pierced sufficiently large for musketry. Two strong bastions, built of logs, commanded the four sides of the square; each bastion had two stories, in which a number of chosen men slept every night. A six-pounder was placed in the lower story, and they were well provided with small arms.

"Immediately in front of the fort was a gentle declivity sloping down to the river's side, which had been turned into an excellent kitchen garden; and a few hundred yards to the left a tolerable wharf had been run out, by which bateaux and boats were enabled at low water to land their cargoes without sustaining any damage. An impenetrable forest of gigantic pines rose in the rear; and the ground was covered with a thick underwood of brier and huckleberry, intermingled with fern and honeysuckle."

When Fort Astoria began to stir with renewed activity in the late spring of 1812, it was agreed that Hunt would make an exact commercial survey of the coast. Robert Stuart, with papers to replace those stolen from Reed, was to cross the continent with two dissatisfied partners who made up their minds to return to the United States, and John Clarke and company were fitted out with an assortment of merchandise to create a new

establishment on the Spokane or Clarke's River. Others were destined for the borders
of the Lewis (Snake) River, while David Stuart was to explore the region lying north of
his post at Okanagan. Outfitted with canoes, boatmen, and hunters, the flotilla left Astoria
with sixty-two men on June 30, 1812.

Assigned to Clarke's expedition to the Spokane, Cox embarked on his first wilderness adventure. It took a month to reach the Walla Walla River, where Robert Stuart's small detachment left the main party. A few days later, at the confluence of the Snake River, "David
Stuart and a party proceeded in their canoes up the Columbia to the trading establishment
which he had formed at Okanagan River. Donald McKenzie and his party proceeded up the
[Snake] river in order to establish a trading post on the upper parts of it, or in the country
of the Snake Indians; his choice to be augmented according to the appearance of beaver in
either place."

Cox's party, led by Clarke, set off for the "Spokan tribe of Indians," about one hundred fifty
miles northeast of the Snake. While yet in the neighborhood of the Snake, the party came
to an area where "the ground is covered with loose grass and abounds in great quantities
of the prickly-pear, the thorns of which are remarkably sharp, and strong enough to penetrate
the leather of the thickest moccasins." The eighteen-year-old Cox was "riding a short distance
ahead of the men [when] my horse happened to stand on a bunch of the prickly-pears, which
pained him so much that he commenced plunging and kicking, and ultimately threw me into
a cluster of them. My face, neck, and body were severely pierced; and every effort to rise only
increased the painfulness of my situation, for whenever I placed my hands to assist in raising
my body, they came in contact with the same tormenting thorns. In fact I could not move an
inch; and to add to my disaster, I observed three rattlesnakes within a few feet of my head.
The men who were in the rear driving the horses, hearing my cries, quickly came to my assistance, and with considerable difficulty disentangled me from my painful situation; the snakes
in the mean time had disappeared. I immediately hailed the canoes, and resumed my old place
on board, firmly resolved never again to ride while a prickly-pear was visible."

A BEND ON THE SNAKE RIVER

Clarke now went about selecting a spot for a trading post and decided on a site at the junction of the Spokane and Coeur d'Alene Rivers, "close to a trading post of the North-West Company, under the command of Mr. McMillan. He had two other posts detached from this: one about two hundred and forty miles from it in a north-easterly direction among a tribe called the Flat-heads, whose lands lie at the feet of the Rocky Mountains, and are well stocked with buffaloes; the other about two hundred miles nearly due north, among a tribe called the Cootonais [Kootenays] in whose country there are plenty of beavers, deer, mountain sheep, and at times, buffaloes. Mr. Finan McDonald of the North-West Company had charge of the post among the Flat-heads; and a Mr. Montour was stationed among the Cootonais. Mr. Pillet was despatched with six men to oppose the latter; and Farnham and I were destined for the Flat-heads."

Cox, Farnham, and their small detachment reached the Flathead country three weeks later and built a small trading post. They next made their way back to the Spokane post and were joined there early in the spring by Farnham and Pillet "returning from their winter posts" among the Kootenays. "Their success exceeded our anticipations. Both Flatheads and Kootenays made excellent winter hunts, and returned in the spring loaded with beaver." A contretemps arose between the Astorian Pillet and the North-Wester Montour. The men fought a duel "with pocket pistols, at six paces; both hits; one in the collar of the coat, and the other in the leg of the trousers. The tailor speedily healed their wounds."

It was not until mid-January 1813 that the Astorians learned about the declaration of war by the United States against Great Britain. (The war had begun officially in June of the prior year.) After considerations including their being, almost to a man, British subjects, and the improbability of Astor's being able to send supplies or reinforcements for the war's duration, the group decided to abandon Fort Astoria in the spring.

Wilson Hunt, on returning from an extended voyage "was surprised beyond measure," according to Gilbert Franchere, a Montrealer who had come to Fort Astoria on the *Tonquin*, and had helped establish the Fort, "when we informed him of the resolution we had taken of abandoning the country." But the other partners were adamant; Hunt had to yield to their decision.

In October, Franchere reports, "the gentlemen of the North West Company took possession of Astoria. The American colors were hauled down and the British run up, to the no small chagrin and mortification of those who were American citizens." Soon after, Fort Astoria became Fort George.

Alexander Ross, a Scot who joined the Astorians at the age of twenty-seven, chronicles the finale: "We have now brought together the accounts of all the different and widely extended branches of the concern. That concern which proposed to extend its grasping influence from ocean to ocean, and which to use [John Jacob Astor's] own words, 'was to have annihilated the South Company; rivalled the North-West Company; extinguished the Hudson's Bay Company; driven the Russians into the Frozen Ocean; and with the resources of China to have enriched America.' But how vain are the designs of man! That undertaking which but yesterday promised such mighty things is today no more."

Stuart, back in 1812

Robert Stuart kept a diary entitled Journal of a Voyage across the Continent from Astoria, *which was provided by John Jacob Astor to Washington Irving as source material for* Astoria. *The original journal itself was not published in its entirety until 1933, when it was meticulously edited, along with Stuart's* Traveling Memoranda, *by Philip Ashton Rollins. What follows is based on the Irving narrative and on the Rollins edition.*

Chapter 4

ROBERT STUART: FIRST TO BLAZE THE OREGON TRAIL

While Fort Astoria was falling, Robert Stuart, unaware of the British takeover, was leading his small party of Astorians eastward on his assignment to bring John Jacob Astor reports and financial accountings, already outdated, of his ill-fated Pacific Fur Company.

Accompanying Stuart at the start of the trek were six veterans of Hunt's westward expedition. The men left Fort Astoria three months before the British took possession, planning to travel as far as the Walla Walla River in the company of the three groups which had been dispatched to ascend the Columbia on various trading assignments.

The party accomplished the difficult portages around the rapids of the lower Columbia, and at the confluence of the Walla Walla, friendly Indians came out in a welcoming force. This was the tribe that had previously "succored Crooks and Day at the time of their extremity."

On June 31, "Mr. Stuart and his little band mounted their steeds and took a farewell of their fellow travellers, who gave them three cheers as they set out on their dangerous journey," and, after a day of dreadful thirst, came to the Umatilla River (near today's Pendleton, Oregon), where the men who had struggled westward with Hunt had also found water after crossing the Blue Mountains.

THE SNAKE RIVER IN IDAHO

From here, they set forth over the mountains, climbing over rocks, bluffs and precipices to emerge into Grande Ronde Valley. By the 12th of August they arrived at the Snake River (Idaho) where that "mad river" enters Seven Devils Canyon.

Their next objective was the Caldron Linn farther up the river. They were planning to open the caches left behind by Hunt and retrieve the goods he had been forced to abandon after leaving the un-navigable river. In what appeared to be an unusually fortunate coincidence, they ran into the Shoshone Indian who had guided the Hunt party to Fort Henry the year before and who now offered to take them across the Rocky Mountains via a much shorter and easier route than the one Hunt had taken.

The following day in another extraordinary coincidence, they came upon four of Hunt's former companions vainly trying to catch fish in the river: Joseph Miller, Jacob Rezner, John Hoback, and Edward Robinson. "The haggard looks and naked condition of these men proved how much they had suffered" during the previous winter.

"Nothing could exceed their joy on thus meeting with their old comrades, or the heartiness with which they were welcomed. All hands immediately encamped, and the slender stores of the party were ransacked to furnish out a suitable regale. The next morning they all set out together; Mr. Miller and his comrades having resolved to give up the life of a trapper and accompany Mr. Stuart back to St. Louis."

The ten men continued along the course of the Snake River, and at Salmon Falls they watched Shoshones catching "incredible quantities as the fish attempt to shoot the falls." When they arrived at the Caldron Linn they saw the wreck of Crooks' canoe tossed high among the rocks, but the river bank was too "high and precipitous" for them to attempt its retrieval. They found the site of the caches and discovered that six of them had been opened and rifled. Three, however, were untouched, and in them they found "a few dry goods, some ammunition, and a number of beaver traps."

Hoback, Robinson, and Rezner, despite the disasters that had previously dogged them, now decided that they would take the beaver traps and try their luck one more time, "on the river below Henry's Fort, as they preferred that to returning in their present ragged condition to civilized society." Miller, however, had had enough, and "he adhered to his determination to keep on with the party to St. Louis, and to return to the bosom of civilized society." Miller now presumed to guide the party eastward. He claimed to be familiar with the territory as a result of his trapping explorations, and he said that he could show Stuart a better route through the mountains, one that would be easier to traverse and would avoid the neighborhoods of the dangerous Blackfeet Indians. "He proved, however, but an indifferent guide, and soon they became bewildered among rugged hills and unknown streams, and burnt and barren prairies." Leaving the Snake River in the vicinity of American Falls, they followed the Portneuf River to the Bear River, which Stuart named Miller's River in honor of their guide.

FOOTHILLS IN OREGON

A few days later, their horses were stolen in a daring attack by Crow Indians. The party was forced to continue on foot.

Washington Irving: "Few reverses in this changeful world are more complete and disheartening than that of a traveller, suddenly unhorsed in the midst of the wilderness. Our unfortunate travellers contemplated their situation, for a time, in perfect dismay. A long journey over rugged mountains and immeasurable plains lay before them, which they must painfully perform on foot, and everything necessary for subsistence or defense must be carried on their shoulders. Their dismay, however, was but transient, and they immediately set to work, with that prompt expediency produced by the exigencies of the wilderness, to fit themselves for the change in their condition."

The men re-packed their baggage into loads that could be carried on their backs, burying or throwing into the river whatever they could not carry, "to prevent the villains benefiting more by us."

To this point, in southeastern Idaho, Stuart had blazed what was to become a section of the Oregon Trail. Now, however, Stuart headed northward, along Gray's River in western Wyoming, returning to the Snake River west of the Hoback River. He next turned westward on the Snake River (back into Idaho). Some historians feel that this was, as Hiram Chittenden put it, "a great mistake of the returning overland expedition," that the men, lost and befuddled, had "forgotten that the sun rises in the east."

Stuart spent five weeks traveling a distance, to the mouth of the Hoback River, that would have taken only six days had he turned eastward. Stuart's journals, however, indicate that he descended the Snake River deliberately to avoid further encounters with the Crows, that he really believed Miller was guiding the party to a better route across the mountains,

THE TETON PASS IN WYOMING

and that he hoped to come across bands of Shoshone Indians from whom he could procure replacement horses.

Several weeks later, having struggled eastward across the Teton Pass, the Gros Ventre Range, and the southeastern base of the Wind River Mountains with little more than the flesh of an old run-down buffalo bull to eat, they came upon a camp of Shoshone Indians at East Fork River. The Indians were "poor but hospitable in the extreme, and for a pistol, a breechclout, an axe, a knife, a tin cup, two awls, and a few beads they gave us the only horse they had; and for a few trinkets we got some buffalo meat and leather for moccasins, an article we much want."

The Shoshones informed Stuart that a large force of Crow Indians was encamped in a valley somewhat to the east. To avoid them, Stuart headed in a southeasterly direction. This was a momentous and historic detour in that it brought the party to a southern section of what came to be known as South Pass, a corridor about twenty miles wide, in later years much traversed by trappers, explorers, and westward-bound emigrants. (South Pass, a broad, gently sloping valley, crossed the Continental Divide at a point midway between Independence on the Missouri and Fort Vancouver on the Pacific.)

The men had successfully negotiated the Rocky Mountains, and came through an arid area to the south which they found, as future travelers would find, barren, sandy, and in the summer, almost unbearably hot. They finally entered the fertile valley of the Sweetwater River, one which afforded "excellent pasture for the numerous herds of buffalo with which it abounded."

Following the Sweetwater, and now traveling squarely on the future Oregon Trail, they came to the spectacular Upper Platte Canyon of the North Platte River, which surpassed "in savage grandeur" all the sights they had previously seen. Stuart described the Canyon as "a channel torn through red piles of rocks by which the stream is obstructed and broken, till it comes to a very steep descent of such dreadful depth that we were naturally inclined to turn aside our eyes." Stuart named this the "Fiery Narrows."

On November 1, Stuart "reached a considerable mountain" (Red Buttes, some 15 miles southwest of Casper, Wyoming). The party encamped a few miles farther down the river, where Stuart held a consultation with his men. "All were convinced that it was in vain to attempt prosecuting the voyage on foot at this inclement season of the year through such an extensive Prairie Country where the procuring of fuel was extremely precarious.

"Therefore as it was the universal voice that we must undoubtedly winter somewhere on this side of the Missouri, I deemed it highly imprudent to go any lower, as it would endanger our safety without the least probable benefit to the expedition; more particularly as our encampment is a situation possessing all the necessary requisites, for here we have wood in abundance both for building and firewood, and the country around is plentifully stocked with game. We have determined on passing the winter here and will leave it on the opening of the navigation in one or perhaps two buffalo-hide canoes, till which time we entertain strong hopes of living in peace and quiet."

For six weeks their hopes of living in peace were realized, but in mid-December, the calm was abruptly shattered. "Relying with confidence on the snugness of our retreat which from its isolated situation we supposed sufficiently concealed to elude even the prying investigation of Indian spies, we were astonished and confounded at hearing the savage yelp this morning in the vicinity of our hut." Twenty-three Arapaho Indians had come upon their retreat.

The Indians "all ate voraciously and departed peaceably, carrying with them a great proportion of our best meat in which we willingly acquiesced." Stuart's party set to work dressing buffalo skins for use as moccasins "to withstand the severity of the weather," and

SUNRISE ON THE PLATTE RIVER

then resumed the journey eastward. They covered a distance of 330 miles in the following two weeks, bearing away from the mountains and onto the wide prairie, until they came to the North Platte River again, at the site of Torrington, Wyoming, near the Nebraska border. There, on the last day of 1812, they "took up residence" in their second winter quarters.

In early March, "the river having been open for several days and the weather promising a continuation of the thaw, we dragged our canoes [built during the winter] and prepared them" for the descent of the Platte. Stuart was unaware that stretches of the Platte, though wide, were very shallow and clogged with sandbars. A week of dragging and wading brought them only a few miles downstream, and Stuart abandoned the canoes.

Once more trekking on foot, the party came to the confluence of the North and South Platte, then followed the Platte past Grand Island to the Missouri. At the village of the Otoe Indians, Stuart learned that "there was a war between the United States and England, and in fact it had existed for a whole year." Obtaining a canoe from the Otoes, the party paddled down to Fort Osage where they "were very hospitably entertained." On April 30, 1813, "a little before sunset we reached the town of St. Louis all in the most perfect health after a voyage of ten months from Astoria during which time we underwent many dangers, hardships and fatigues, in short I may say, all the privations human nature is capable of." Their return "caused quite a sensation," for it had been about two years since any word had been heard of the men who had gone west in the venture launched by John Jacob Astor.

So, the saga of the Astorians was over. The venture had ended, like that of Manuel Lisa's, in commercial failure—but in successful exploration. Wilson Hunt's trek westward, the Astorians' reconnoitering of the upper Columbia and the future state of Washington, and Robert Stuart's trek eastward are among the greatest explorations in American history. And with their discovery of the Oregon Trail, they opened the gateway to the Far West.

The route traveled by Robert Stuart in leading his party from Fort Astoria to St. Louis, although not designated as the "Oregon Trail" until twenty years later, would become America's vital artery from the East to the Pacific Northwest. Its eastern portion, from the Missouri to the Rockies, would be the path taken by emigrants on their way to California as well.

The Oregon Trail would become, during the peak years of western emigration beginning three decades later, as historian Hiram Chittenden described it, "a major national highway two thousand miles in length, a scene of romance, adventure, pleasure and excitement." But this glorious "national highway" was, when first traveled by emigrants, as Chittenden also noted, "a highway of desolation, strewn with abandoned property, the skeletons of horses, mules, and oxen, and alas! too often with freshly made mounds and head-boards that told the pitiful tale of sufferings too great to be endured. It was marked in every mile of its course by human misery, tragedy, and death."

The trail began at the future site of Kansas City. This was originally the small town of Independence, but the changing course of the erratic Missouri River destroyed its landing and forced a move to nearby Westport. It crossed the Kansas River at the site of Topeka, Kansas, crossed the Big Sandy at the Kansas-Nebraska line, and reached the Platte below Grand Island. It reached the North Fork of the Platte at Ash Creek and then proceeded (in southwest Nebraska) along the river past Court House Rock, Chimney Rock, and Scott's Bluff. At the confluence of the Laramie River (beyond the Wyoming border), where Fort Laramie was built in 1834, the trail, along the North Platte, entered mountain country.

SCOTT'S BLUFF, NEBRASKA

More than a hundred miles westward it passed Red Buttes, the Fiery Narrows, and at Independence Rock, just beyond where the North Platte bends southward in its descent from Colorado, came to the valley of the Sweetwater River. It passed Devil's Gate, entering a hundred-mile stretch of dry, alkaline terrain, alleviated only by the Sweetwater, leading to the South Pass. The seventy-mile stretch beyond South Pass to the Green River continued dry, barren, and sandy.

The Trail came to Black's Fork of the Green, where Fort Bridger was built, in 1843, by veteran mountain man James Bridger, then entered Utah and came to the Bear River, a stream providing pleasant passage through mountainous country. It followed the Bear River into Idaho and came to the Portneuf, at whose junction with the Snake another famous fort, Fort Hall, was to be built in 1834 by Nathaniel Wyeth. Here, Oregon-bound travelers prepared for the last leg of the journey to the Columbia, and California-bound travelers turned southwestward. (Some also turned at Fort Bridger.)

The Oregon Trail followed the Snake River to today's Glenn Ferry, which it crossed to head on to the Boise River. It next crossed the Malheur River in Oregon, the Burnt River, the Powder River, and entered the Grande Ronde Valley. Then came the difficult crossing of the Blue Mountains, the Umatilla River, and finally the Columbia. Its terminal stretch was along the left bank of the Columbia past the John Day River, Des Chutes River, the Dalles, the Cascades and finally arrived at Fort Vancouver, the Hudson's Bay Company post opposite the mouth of the Willamette, the end of the Oregon Trail.

For several decades the two-thousand-mile route would see nothing but uninhabited wilderness, bands of roaming Indians, and three trading-posts: Fort Laramie, built in 1834, Fort Hall in 1834, and Fort Bridger in 1843.

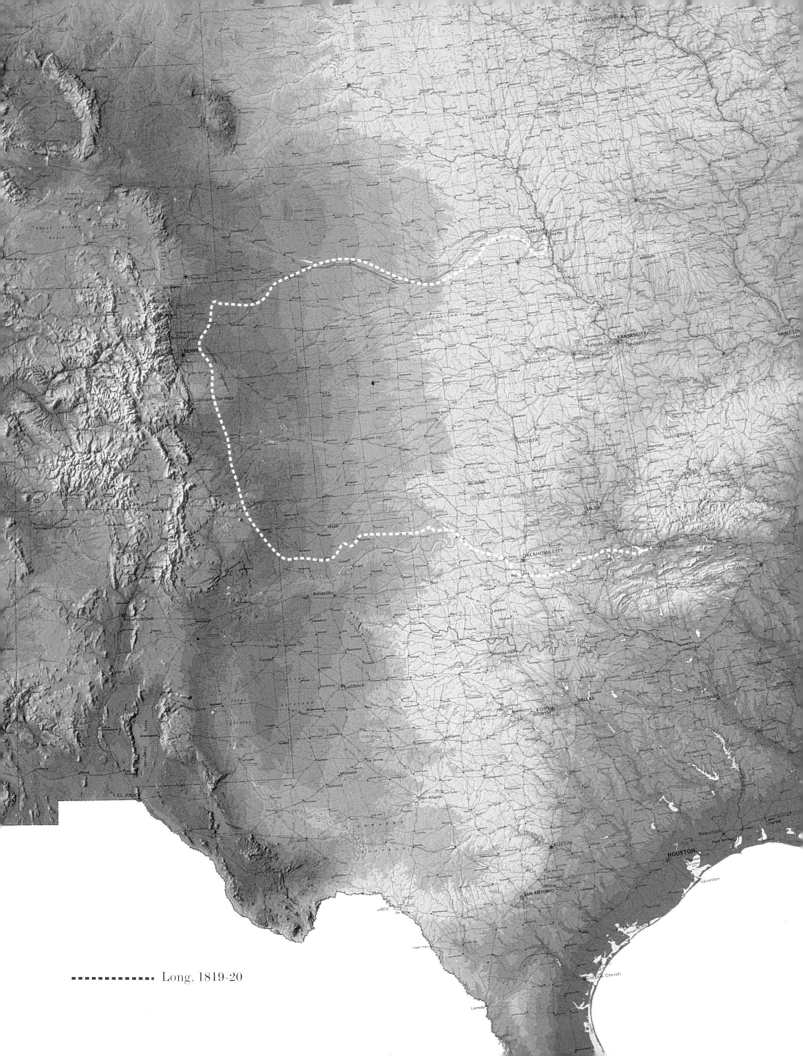

Long, 1819-20

Stephen Long was a graduate of Dartmouth, an engineer, an instructor of mathematics at West Point, and an experienced explorer. He wrote A General Description of the Country Traversed by the Exploring Expedition.

Among those who accompanied him on his southwest expedition were Dr. Edwin James, botanist, geologist, and surgeon, who described what happened in his Account of an Expedition from Pittsburg to the Rocky Mountains, *and Captain John Bell, who wrote* Journal of an Expedition to the foot of the Rocky Mountains near the head waters of the LaPlatte and Arkansas rivers. *Edwin James, born in Vermont, graduated from Middlebury College, and studied medicine, botany, and geology at Albany, New York. In his erudite and literate journal he included observations made by Major Long and by the expedition's zoologist, Dr. Thomas Say.*

Chapter 5

MAJOR STEPHEN LONG'S SOUTHWEST EXPEDITION

The fall of Astoria, the nation's involvement with the three-year War of 1812, the post-war economic boom, America's preoccupation with affairs east of the Mississippi, and a disastrous expedition to the Upper Missouri in 1819 halted exploration of the West from the return of the Astorians until 1820.

In that year, Major Stephen Long, co-commander of a failed attempt to reassert American dominance in the area of the Upper Missouri, was instructed to lead his scientific corps to the Southwest in order to explore "the source of the River Platte in the mountains and thence by way of the Arkansas and Red Rivers to the Mississippi." Major Long would survey the presumed borderline between the Louisiana Territory of the United States and the colonial territories of Spain.

Twenty-two poorly equipped men left Council Bluffs, Nebraska, on June 6, 1820, under Long's command. For several days they followed an Indian trail to the village of the Grand Pawnees near the Loup river (visited by Zebulon Pike), passing from there to the Republican Pawnees and then the site of the Pawnee Loups.

Photo by W. Ben Glass

A short distance from the Loup River they came to the Platte (near Grand Island, Nebraska), which they had been instructed to ascend to its source. The men were astonished by the immense hordes of buffalo "blackening the whole surface of the country through which we passed. The country along the Platte is enlivened by great numbers of deer, badgers, hares, prairies wolves, eagles, buzzards, ravens and owls; these, with its rare and interesting plants, in some measure relieved the uniformity of its cheerless scenery."

From Grand Island the party followed the future Oregon Trail to the Forks of the Platte in western Nebraska and then left it to ascend the South Fork to Colorado. At the end of June they were "cheered by a distant view of the Rocky mountains. Snow could be seen on every part of them which was visible above our horizon." Six days later, after passing to the west of today's Denver, they "arrived at the boundary of the vast plain across which we had held our weary march for a distance of near one thousand miles and encamped at the base of the mountain. Our camp was immediately in front of the chasm through which the Platte issues from the mountains.

"The design of the party had been to cross the first range of mountains and gain the valley of the Platte beyond, but this they found themselves unable to accomplish. After climbing successively to the summit of several ridges which they had supposed to be the top of the mountain, they still found others beyond higher and more rugged. They therefore relinquished the intention of crossing." (Major Long thus aborted his assignment of ascending the Platte to its source.) After leaving Platte Canyon they came to a location near today's Colorado Springs where "they had a distinct view of the part of the mountains called by Captain Pike the highest peak." Dr. Edwin James, botanist, geologist, and surgeon, decided that he would attempt to climb it.

On July 13, James and two companions began their climb, finding "the surface in many places covered with such quantities of loose and crumbled granite, rolling from under their feet, as rendered the ascent extremely difficult. Though many attempts had been made by the Indians and by hunters to ascend, none had ever proved successful. After laboring with extreme fatigue over about two miles, in which several of these dangerous places occurred, we halted at sunset in a small cluster of fir trees. We could not, however, find a piece of even ground large enough to lie down upon, and were under the necessity of securing ourselves from rolling into the brook near which we encamped by means of a pole placed against two trees. In this situation we passed an uneasy night."

In the morning they "found the way less difficult and dangerous. A little above the point where the timber disappears entirely commences a region of astonishing beauty. The intervals of soil are sometimes extensive, and covered with a carpet of low but brilliantly-flowered alpine plants. It was about 4 o'clock PM when [we] arrived on the summit. From there the view towards the north-west and south-west is diversified with innumerable mountains, all white with snow. To the east lay the green plain. The Arkansas with several of its tributaries, and some of the branches of the Platte, could be distinctly traced as on a map. On the south the mountain is continued, having another summit, supposed to be that ascended by Captain Pike."

Major Long paid tribute to the achievement, the first ascent of the peak, by naming it James Peak, but the name did not endure; it became known as Pike's Peak, after the man who first spotted it.

After this, the Long expedition turned southward to the Red River while a party led by Captain John Bell was dispatched to explore the Arkansas. "We turned our backs upon the mountains [but] it was not without a feeling of something like regret that we found our long contemplated visit to these grand and interesting objects was now at and end."

(A West Point graduate who had served in the War of 1812 and subsequently became Commandant of Cadets and Instructor of Infantry Tactics at the military academy, Bell had requested assignment to the Long expedition and became its "official journalist.")

On July 25, 1820, the Bell party's second day of march along the river in southeast Colorado, "a considerable number of Indians had assembled to see us, apparently of different nations [they were Kiowas, Cheyennes, Kaskayas and Arapahos] who were some what inquisitive in their inquiries, of who we were, the place we came from and the objects of [our] tour through the country."

Indians abounded in this area, and when Bell's party crossed today's Colorado-Kansas state line they met a war party of Cheyennes. "Some of them were painted black and had a most horrid frightful appearance," but no hostility was displayed by them. "We rode off congratulating ourselves at the happy issues of our meeting with a Cheyenne war-party, the most to be dreaded and feared of all other nations."

Passing the future site of Dodge City, Bell became confused about the geography of the region. He thought he had arrived at the Great Bend of the Arkansas; he was far south of it. Then he thought he had passed the Little Arkansas tributary; he was wrong.

The mid-August heat on the Kansas plains was oppressive. Bell's party was marching through "the face of a country so level that it is with difficulty we can designate objects by which we can take our courses; the river is so meandering that its course thro the plain can not be seen more than a mile, and we have to follow along its bank, crooked as it is, lest we should get too far off. How much anxiety of feeling would have been saved to us had we but a map of this country with us. Pike's map would have furnished us with such a knowledge of the country as at least to have enabled us to judge in which part of it we were."

At the site of today's Wichita, Kansas, they discovered "an old Indian village, or may more likely be, an Indian hunting camp for the winter season, as many of the cabins were enclosed and covered with bark; in and about them was growing water melons, pumpkin and corn." Soon they arrived at a river which Bell thought was the Verdigris. He was "sadly disappointed at not meeting with the Osage Indians," which would have signified that they were on course and on schedule. But they were at Walnut Creek; the confluence of the Verdigris was many miles ahead, entering the Arkansas near today's Muskogee, Oklahoma.

The next tributary they came to was Grouse Creek, near today's Kansas-Oklahoma state line, and this Bell mistook for the Grand, or Neosho, River. "We cannot account for the absence of Indians, which we were told we should find on the rivers we have just crossed, for we have neglected to supply ourselves with meat more than to serve us to this place, where we expected to obtain some from the Indians."

Bell climbed a hill and saw from the summit that the country ahead appeared "broken and cut up with deep ravines." They were obliged to trek through the difficult terrain, marching for days without food.

Bell and his party then headed toward a large river "which we supposed to be the Illinois." Descending to cross the river, however, "I discovered to my great mortification that it was the Arkansas. I then discovered that the river instead of coming from the north came in from the south and at its confluence with the Arkansas that river made a short turn to the left, which I had mistaken for the Illinois." (This was the Nebraska, or Salt River, a tributary of the Arkansas; Bell was two hundred miles distant from the Illinois.)

On August 28 they "struck upon a well beaten trace which we followed along down the margin of the river. We believed it to head directly to Belle Point" (the destination Major Long had chosen for the parties' reunion). It didn't, and they ended up taking a detour that missed the important Arkansas tributary, the Cimarron, before returning to the river.

Their frustrating, trouble-plagued expedition was coming to an end. Seven days after meeting a member of the Osage tribe, they arrived at Belle Point, greatly relieved to have made it, and considered their muddled effort "completely successful."

Long's party, in the meantime, had departed on a circuitous course which led them through country containing "precipitous ramparts . . . abrupt conic piles, narrow ridges, . . . shapeless fragments of naked rocks . . . (and) perpendicular cliffs of red sandstone."

"With some difficulty" they crossed the Cimarron, a river of "transparent and nearly pure water" and came to a "barren and desolate region [the Panhandle of Oklahoma] affording no game and nearly destitute of wood and water." Violent storms and tortuous trails were hard on them, and on their horses.

Mistaking a stream in the Texas Panhandle for a tributary of the Red River, the travelers, endlessly annoyed by blow flies, gnats, mosquitoes, and ticks, "the most tormenting of the insects of this country," were further disheartened when they realized they should long before have reached their destination.

On September 10, when the party found itself unmistakably on the Arkansas River, they knew their mission had failed. The river Long had followed was the Canadian, which flows eastward considerably to the north of the Red River. Major Long's expedition ended when his party rejoined Bell's at Belle Point.

Despite its blunders, its failures to meet its prescribed objectives, and Long's mistaken conclusions that the country was uninhabitable, the Long expedition had some successes and achievements. It was the first to ascend Pike's Peak, to explore the Canadian River, and to reconnoiter unknown sections of the Southwest. Its most important contributions, however, were those of its scientists in extending knowledge of the Southwest's botany, zoology, geology, and ethnology.

The negative observations Long made about the Southwest furthered the unfortunate notion, originated by Zebulon Pike, that it constituted a "great American desert" and contributed heavily to the American government's indifference to further exploration of, or expansion into, the West.

It would be years before that indifference would be overcome by the persistence of Americans who would not be dissuaded from moving westward, and whose protection would become a national priority.

LOOKING WEST FROM THE SUMMIT OF PIKE'S PEAK

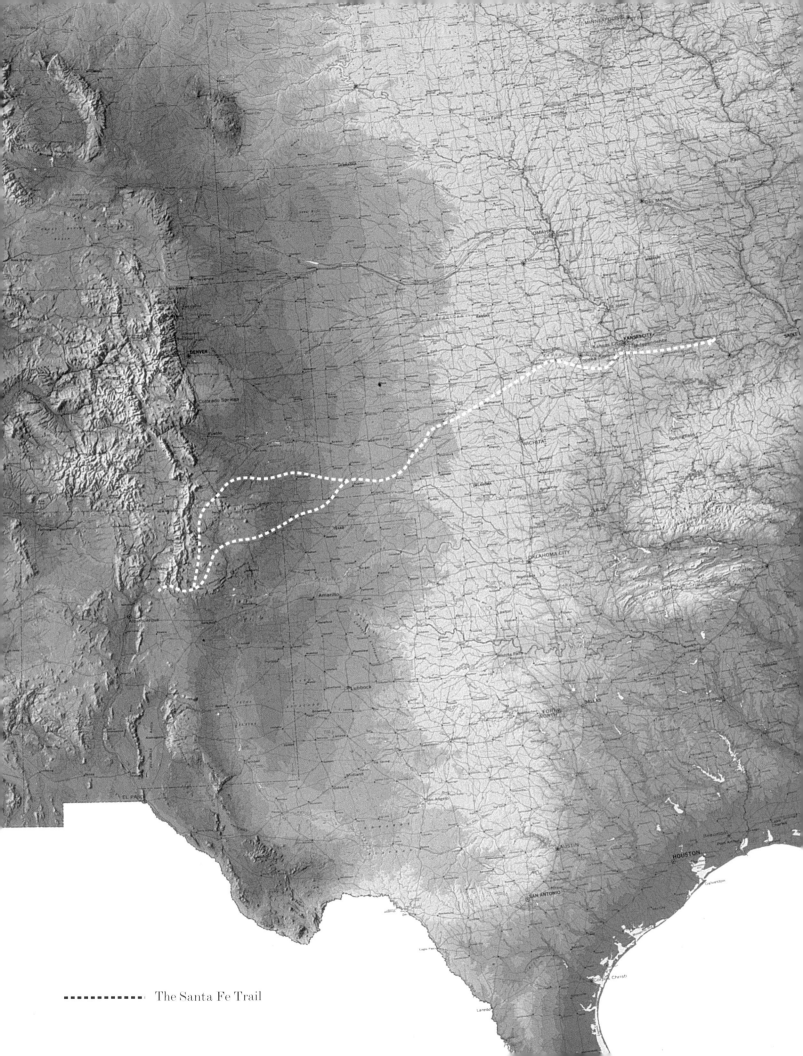

- - - - - - - - - - - - - The Santa Fe Trail

The journals of Thomas James and Jacob Fowler, narrating the events of these pioneering days in the Santa Fe trade, along with the difficulties of the trek across the barren lands of the Southwest, are the sources of this chapter.

Thomas James told the story of his Santa Fe and Upper Missouri adventures in Three Years among the Indians and Mexicans.

The source for the narrative of the Glenn-Fowler expedition is Fowler's Memorandum of the voige by land from fort Smith to the Rocky mountains. *Fowler's spelling and grammar were so grotesquely difficult that his journal remained unpublished and unedited until 1898 when the scholarly historian of the West, Elliot Coues, undertook the challenge.*

Chapter 6

JAMES AND FOWLER: THE OPENING OF THE SANTA FE TRAIL

The discouraging descriptions of the southwest portion of the Louisiana Territory provided by Stephen Long and Zebulon Pike dissuaded all but the most adventurous from attempting passage of this barren and inhospitable wilderness. But beyond the Louisiana Territory, beyond the borderline of the United States in a land possessed by Spain, lay Santa Fe, where, for those intrepid enough to make their way to it, great profits in trade could be had.

In response to this lure, in defiance of the perilous journey, and with indifference to their intrusion of a foreign power's domain, traders began to make their way to Santa Fe soon after Pike's return. They met with disaster.

Between 1809 and 1821, groups of travelers, trappers, and traders were imprisoned, had their property confiscated, and were ordered to leave Spanish territory. It was not until 1821, when three separate parties had the audacity to enter this territory little knowing what might await them, that the Santa Fe trade finally opened. In November of that year, fate was kind to a pioneering party led by William Becknell of Franklin, Missouri. Arriving in Santa Fe, he was received "with apparent pleasure and joy." Mexico had won its independence from Spain. American traders were welcome! On his return trip, Becknell was the first to travel along the Cimarron River.

When he returned the following year he made the trip with wagons. He is described by some historians as "the father of the Santa Fe Trail." The second party to reach Santa Fe in 1821 was led by Thomas James, the third by Hugh Glenn and Jacob Fowler. Thomas James, who had been on the ill-fated Lisa expedition and faced bankruptcy on his return, decided to accompany John McKnight, who "desired to go to Mexico to see his brother [Robert], procure his release if he were still in prison, and return with him to the States."

The party of eleven departed from St. Louis on May 10, 1821. They descended the Mississippi in a keelboat to the Arkansas River, then ascended to Little Rock, where James procured "a license to trade with all the Indian tribes on the Arkansas and its tributaries." Beyond Little Rock the party "passed through the country of the Cherokees, whose farms and log houses made a fine appearance on the banks of the river [which] would compare favorably with those of any Western state." (At that time no state lay west of the Mississippi.) When the party arrived at Fort Smith, "we tried to mark out our course for the future, which we determined should be the Arkansas to within sixty miles from Taos in New Mexico." The Arkansas River was, James found, too shallow for further navigation, so the party bought horses from the Osages and proceeded overland to the banks of the Cimarron. They followed the Cimarron for three weeks through arid Oklahoma "over mounds and between hills of sand which the wind had blown up in some places to a height of one hundred feet. Our progress was very slow, the horses sometimes sinking to their breasts in the sand."

In the Panhandle of Oklahoma the party left the Cimarron to strike the North Fork of the Canadian River. They then turned into the Panhandle of Texas and stopped to hunt buffalo. Not many days later they were captured by Comanches who marched James and his men to the Indian encampment where "about a thousand chiefs and warriors surrounded us. I laid out for them tobacco, powder, lead, vermillion, calico and other articles." This did not satisfy them and on the fourth day, "we . . . learned that our deaths were determined upon."

After a dramatic rescue by Spanish cavalrymen who brought the news of the Mexican Revolution and the Indians' independence, the party was guided along the Canadian River across eastern New Mexico to the mountains.

The Ruins of Jemez Mission near the springs west of Santa Fe

From the Canadian the travelers proceeded to the Pecos River at the town of La Cuesta, and from there to San Miguel (subsequently an important spot on the Santa Fe Trail), and on to the town of Pecos. On December 1, 1821, the party "came in sight of Santa Fe, which presented a fine appearance in the distance. It is beautifully situated on a plain of dry and rolling ground, at the foot of the high mountain, and a small stream which rises in the mountain to the west runs directly through the city."

In Santa Fe, Thomas James received permission "to vend my goods," but his trading business fared badly "on account of the scarcity of money." John McKnight learned that his brother had been released from prison by the newly independent Mexicans, and had gone to live in Durango, Mexico, where John found him and brought him back to Santa Fe.

His business failing, James, bitterly frustrated, abandoned his attempts at trade with the Mexicans, sold some of his goods to Hugh Glenn, who "wanted the goods to sell to his company who were trapping near Taos [under Jacob Fowler's leadership], and promised to pay the money as soon as he reached St. Louis and disposed of his beaver fur. Taking him for a man of honor I treated him as such, to my own loss." James left Santa Fe in June 1822, and returned only once more in his career as a trader.

Years later when he wrote his reminiscences, James noted that "there are three principal routes over the mountains to New Mexico. One below San Miguel, by which I went to Santa Fe [a leg of the Santa Fe Trail], and which is easily passable for a large army without a danger of surprise. The second, through which I was now returning to the States [a new route which failed to become part of the Trail], and the third, a few miles to the north of this [through the Raton Pass], which will probably become the great outlet of American emigration to California."

The hapless trader, having had his horses stolen from him, was back in St. Louis late in July. "My creditors swarmed around me like bees, and were as clamorous as a drove of hungry wolves." His associate in the Santa Fe venture, John McKnight, then "proposed to make another venture among the Comanches." James agreed and, in the fall, he, John McKnight, Robert McKnight, and a party of eight ascended the North Fork of the Canadian River, traversing the northern portion of the Cross Timbers of Oklahoma.

James commented that the area, "though designated as the Great American Desert is very different from those plains of sand in the Old World which bear that name. A short grass grows here, but no timber except the cottonwood and willows in the bends of the rivers."

At a site in northwest Oklahoma the party erected a fort as its trading post. Of those who ventured out to find the Comanches, John McKnight died at their hands and two of his companions were taken hostage. James loaded four mules with goods, and in the company of a band of Wichita Indians made his way to the nearby Comanche village. He found that "the hostages were all in safety and had been well treated." But the Comanches were unfriendly and reluctant to trade. James offered the chief two plugs of tobacco. The Comanche "smelled of the tobacco, pressed it to his heart, and raised his head with a smile.

The white man had gained the ascendant. The scene changed and all was friendly welcome where before was nothing but menacing and frowning coldness."

James enjoyed extraordinary success among the Comanches, trading with them "for horses, mules, beaver fur, and buffalo robes. One plug of tobacco, a knife, and a few strings of beads, in all worth little more than a dime, bought one of those valuable skins or robes worth at least five dollars in any of the States!"

James parted from the Comanches and headed homeward. But bad luck continued to plague him. "Then commenced a series of misfortunes and unavoidable accidents which continued till I reached the settlements and which destroyed all hope of profit from the adventure." He lost most of his horses in two stampedes on the prairie. More horses died in the passage through the Cross Timbers. And, the final blow, a member of his party stole the pelts which James had obtained from the Comanches. After so many years of pioneering effort on the Upper Missouri and in the Southwest, James had gained no benefit other than the satisfaction of having survived.

Jacob Fowler was born in New York, came to Kentucky as a young man, and became a government surveyor. His unique spelling and grammar notwithstanding, he was a well-educated and intelligent man. It is not known what motivated him to become a trader and trapper in the Southwest, but the lure of adventure, and the potential of substantial financial gain, had motivated many others.

Fowler's co-commander on the New Mexico expedition was Hugh Glenn, an experienced trader whose post was located at the confluence of the Arkansas and Verdigris rivers near today's Muskogee, Oklahoma. On September 25, 1821, they started their trek to New Mexico.

Like James before them, they followed the Arkansas River, but unlike James they did not leave it to descend the Cimarron, following it instead, as Zebulon Pike had, all the way to Colorado. Their travel along the Arkansas was uneventful. Like James had, they purchased horses at the Osage village near Taos. (Fowler does not mention meeting James there.) On October 31, Fowler noted that along the banks "a great many trees appeer to Have [been] Cut down by White men." A week later: "We again See the Sign of White men a Head of us" (the James party).

On November 13, having reached Colorado, the party "asended a gradual Rise for about three miles to the Highest ground in the nibourhood—Wheare We Head a full vew of the mountains this must be the place Whare Pike first discovered the mountains" (the Spanish Peaks, also known as Wahtoyah and as Las Cumbres Espanolas). That afternoon, when they reached the Purgatoire River, a tragic incident occurred.

"We Heare found some grapes among the brush . . . While Some Ware Hunting and others Cooking Some Picking grapes a gun Was fyered off and the Cry of a White Bare [a grizzly] Was Raised We Ware all armed in an Instent and Each man Run His own Cors to look for the desperet anemel . . .

"The Brush in Which We Camped Contained from 10 to 20 acors Into Which the Bare Head Run for Shelter find Him Self Surrounded on all Sides ... threw this Conl glann With four others atemted to Run But the Bare being In their Way and lay Close in the brush undiscovered till the Ware With in a few feet of it ... When it Sprung up and Caught Lewis doson [Dawson] and Pulled Him down In an Instent ... " The grizzly was finally slain, but too late to save Dawson from a fatal mauling. "It appeers His Head Was In the Bares mouth at least twice ... and that When the monster give the Crush that Was to mash the mans Head it being two large for the Span of His mouth the Head Sliped out only the teeth Cutting the Skin to the bone Where Ever the touched it ... so that the Skin of the Head Was Cut from about the Ears to the top in Several derections ... all of Which Wounds Ware Sewed up as Well as Cold be don by men In our Situation Haveing no Surgen nor Surgical Instruments ... the man Still Retained His under Standing but Said I am killed that I Heard my Skull Brake ... " Dawson died two days later.

The party was then somewhere between La Junta and Pueblo, near the site of the future Bent's Fort, an important junction on the mountain route of the Santa Fe Trail and the Taos Trail, as well as the south-north route between Santa Fe and the Oregon Trail along the Platte River.

A few miles farther west, the men came upon a large band of Kiowa Indians who were making camp on the river bank.

"The hole of this day the Indeans Continu to arive and Set up their lodges ... So that by night We Ware a large town Containing up Wards two Honderd Houses Well filled With men Wemon and Children ... With a great nombr of dogs and Horses So that the Hole Cuntry to a great distance Was Coverd ... this Scenes Was new to us and the more So after our long

81

Bison in the Winter

Jurney Seeing no persons but our Selves…the Indeans Ware frendly takeing us to the lodges of their great men and all Ways Seting Some meat for us to eat.

"The snow Has now Increeced to about 10 Inches deep and the Wind Extreemly Cold the River frosen up Close the Ice to a great thickness." The party decided to remain among the friendly Indians until the weather improved.

Comanches arrived at the camp and threatened the travelers, but soon the encampment became the scene of a great Indian pow-wow. The Arapahos arrived, then bands of Paducahs, and Cheyennes and Snakes. Under the protection of the Arapahos, the Fowler-Glenn party departed from the Indian camp, and moved westward to the Huerfano River. A few days later, an Indian scout reported that sixty Spaniards were heading toward the expedition. They were not alarmed because, although the party was only thirteen men, they felt secure in the midst of the multitude of Arapahos.

As the Spanish and the Glenn-Fowler party approached each other, the Spanish formed in "military style," charged to within ten paces, and then dismounted and "embraced us with affection and friendship."

On January 2, 1822, Glenn and four men joined the Spanish group to "cross the mountains to Santafee," in order to determine whether the party would be permitted to enter and trade while Fowler and the rest remained behind.

Fowler set the men to work building a log house, believed to be the first house built by Americans in Colorado, at a site that was to become the city of Pueblo. During the next fortnight the men busied themselves with attempts at trapping beaver and hunting buffalo while they awaited the return of Hugh Glenn. "We began to Sopose He Is now not at liverty to send or Return there being the full time Elapsed in Which He promised to send an Express…We begin to Conclude [all] Is not Well with Him …"

On January 29, however, a group of Spaniards rode up, escorting one of the men who had previously gone to Santa Fe with Hugh Glenn. They had been sent to "Conduct us to the Spanish Settle ment Wheare the governor and People Head Recd [Glenn] on the most frendly terms."

Fowler and his men now proceeded to cross the Sangre de Cristo range, escorted by the Spanish along the Taos Trail. They were the first Americans to travel this route, which had long been used by Spanish traders. At the Pueblo de Taos, on February 8, they were met by Glenn.

THE RIO GRANDE CUTS THROUGH THE GORGE AT TAOS

Beneficiaries of Mexico's friendly attitude toward American traders, Fowler and a party of trappers spent the next four months trapping beaver in the streams of northern New Mexico and southern Colorado.

But beaver were scarce and the weather severe, with frequent snowstorms. Streams froze, making beaver trapping impossible. Meanwhile, Glenn had spent much time in Santa Fe, but was unsuccessful in developing a profitable trading business.

On June 1, the date predetermined for their departure from New Mexico, the Glenn-Fowler party set off from Taos. "James and mcnights party from Stafee Had Joined ours and all moved on together…" The first leg of the homeward trek was along the route described by James (a route that failed to be used by subsequent travelers on the Santa Fe Trail). They crossed the Sangre de Cristos into southern Colorado, proceeded past the Purgatoire River, and struck the Arkansas River at the Kansas border (near today's town of Coolidge).

On June 12, a few miles farther along the river, "a party of White men appeered on the Same Side…one of them came over to our camp…this was Conl Cooppers party from Boons lick on their Way to the Spanish Settlement With Some goods and Some traps to take Bever."

Stimulated by Becknell's favorable reports, "the commerce of the prairies" had begun. Among the first traders after Becknell, James, Glenn, and Fowler was the man whom Fowler identifies as Braxton Cooper. With Cooper's party was Joseph Walker who, a decade later, would accompany Benjamin Bonneville to the West, and would lead a historic expedition overland to northern California.

After the James-McKnight party separated from them, Fowler and Glenn followed a devious route south of the Arkansas. Fowler wrote: "Like Ship With out a Rudder We Steered from South East to North East. I suppose the gide was lost." When they came to the headwaters of the Verdigris River, they found wagon tracks on the plain—unexpected and astonishing. (The tracks had recently been made by William Becknell's second expedition to Santa Fe, on which he was the first to use wagons on the trail.)

From here, Fowler and Glenn went home. For these two traders, as well as for Thomas James, efforts in the first year of Mexican independence had proved financially unrewarding. Their efforts as pathfinders, however, were notable. William Becknell, the other 1821 adventurer, had enjoyed success both as an explorer and as a trader.

Braxton Cooper went on to establish a good trade. James Baird and Samuel Chambers, who had been imprisoned in New Mexico in 1812, returned to Santa Fe in 1822, and they too established a successful trade. By 1824, the Santa Fe trade was flourishing so prosperously that Thomas Hart Benton, Missouri senator, vigorous advocate of western expansion, and a staunch supporter of his St. Louis fur-trading constituents, persuaded Congress to appropriate funds for surveying and improving the route to Santa Fe.

Eventually, the Santa Fe Trail went from Independence on the Missouri westward (sharing the same path as the Oregon Trail for the first forty miles or so) to Council Grove, and then across the Kansas plains to a point near the confluence of Walnut Creek and the Arkansas River (at Great Bend), and along the river to a point (above Dodge City) where one branch followed the Cimarron Cut-off across desert terrain in the northwest corner of the Oklahoma Panhandle into New Mexico; the other branch, the mountain branch, continued to follow the Arkansas River into Colorado before turning southward at Bent's Fort to enter New Mexico by way of Raton Pass.

Although the terrain was difficult and the Indians dangerous, determined traders would brave the perils of the trail, traveling in large caravans for security. These were the men who would succeed in making the Santa Fe Trail an artery as vital to America's opening of the Southwest as the Oregon Trail was to become to the Northwest.

THE ARKANSAS RIVER IN COLORADO

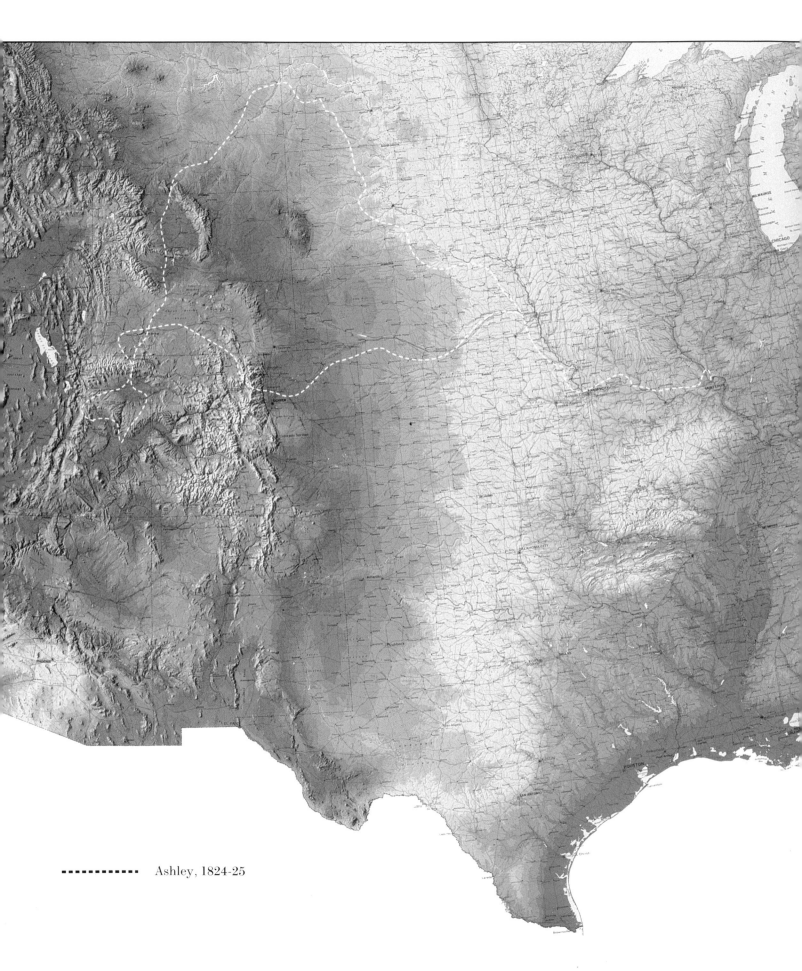

Ashley, 1824-25

The remarkable explorations and accomplishments of the mountain men were chronicled in fragments of journals, letters, and reports written by William Ashley and Jedediah Strong Smith, as well as by some of the men who accompanied them. Several different sources in addition to the original journals themselves were used: Harrison Dale's The Ashley-Smith Explorations and the Discovery of a Central Route to California, *Maurice Sullivan's* The Journals of Jedediah Smith, *Dale Morgan's* Jedediah Smith and the Opening of the West, *Charles Camp's* James Clyman, American Frontiersman, *Leroy Hafen's* Broken Hand, the Life Story of Thomas Fitzpatrick, *Bernard DeVoto's* Across the Wide Missouri, *and Hiram Chittenden's indispensable* The History of the American Fur Trade of the Far West.

Chapter 7

ASHLEY AND SMITH: THE MOUNTAIN MEN CONQUER THE ROCKIES

In less than two decades following the acquisition of the Louisiana Territory, American explorers and traders had opened trails into its vast wilderness, heading southwest into the Spanish settlements of New Mexico and northwest into the unsettled Oregon Country.

They had blazed trails in present-day Kansas, Nebraska, South Dakota, North Dakota, Montana, Wyoming, Idaho, Oregon, and Washington, in Arkansas, Louisiana, Oklahoma, Texas, and New Mexico. But none had yet found a central trail over the Rocky Mountains that led across the wilderness of the future states of Utah, Nevada, and Arizona; and none had made their way to California.

Beginning in 1822 this would change, thanks to two of the greatest American explorer-trappers, William Ashley and Jedediah Strong Smith, and their companions, the celebrated "mountain men" of western America.

After the War of 1812, Andrew Henry (of Henry's Fort on the Snake River) and William Ashley formed a company to trap beaver in the territory beyond the Rockies. Henry had been there; he knew where beaver were abundant.

William Ashley was born in Virginia, moved to St. Louis in 1808, in 1821 was elected lieutenant governor, and in 1822 was appointed general in the militia. Despite these achievements, he had not enjoyed the success he sought in business.

In early spring of 1822, Henry and Ashley, then forty-four, set about organizing a trapping
expedition. Among those who joined him were men who would gain lasting fame: Jedediah
Strong Smith, James Bridger, James Clyman, Thomas Fitzpatrick, Hugh Glass, Joe Meek,
Etienne Provost, Edward Rose, and William Sublette.

The first of the three expeditions it would take before Henry and Ashley were to succeed
left half the party, including Henry and Smith, near the mouth of the Yellowstone. Smith
was then sent to meet Ashley's second expedition, but was lucky to escape with his life from
an Indian attack which took the lives of many of Ashley's party. The determined Ashley
organized a third expedition and, late in 1824, went west again, this time to the country
south of the Upper Missouri and the Yellowstone, following Major Stephen Long's course
to the Rockies along the future Oregon Trail.

He described his journey in a letter to General Henry Atkinson: "I left Fort Atkinson [near
Council Bluffs on the Missouri] on the 3rd November, 1824, and on the 22nd of the same
month we found ourselves encamped on the Loup Fork of the river Platte within three miles
of the Pawnee towns. After ascending the [Platte] about one hundred miles, we reached
Plumb Point [south of today's Kearney, Nebraska] on the 3rd of December, where we found
the encampment of the Grand Pawnee Indians who had reached that point on their route
to the wintering ground on the Arkansas River." The Pawnees advised Ashley "to take up

A BULL BISON

winter quarters at the forks of the Platte," but after three weeks he left the Indians and, with horses and provisions he had purchased from them, proceeded along the South Platte. "The weather was fine, the valleys literally covered with buffaloes, and everything seemed to promise a safe and speedy movement. The snow was now so deep that had it not been for the numerous herds of buffalo moving down the river, we could not possibly have proceeded. The paths of these animals were beat on either side of the river and afforded an easy passage to our horses."

By the end of February Ashley reached the front range of the Rockies. "Our passage across the first range of mountains, which was extremely difficult and dangerous, employed us three days, after which the country presented a different aspect. The ascent of the hills, for they do not deserve the name of mountains, was so gradual as to cause but little fatigue in travelling over them."

THE GREEN RIVER AT DINOSAUR NATIONAL MONUMENT

Book Cliffs in the Green River area, Utah, in early Spring

Beyond the Laramie River the Medicine Bow range seemed too formidable an obstacle, so Ashley moved slowly along its base, his men trapping as they went, until he found a viable pass. "From the morning of the 27th [March] to the night of the 1st April, we were employed in crossing the ridge which divides the waters of the Atlantic from those of the Pacific Ocean." (Ashley and his party were the first Americans to cross the Rockies via what came to be known as Bridger's Pass, somewhat to the south of South Pass.)

On April 18 (at what is now the Seekskadee National Wildlife Refuge) they "came to a beautiful river running South." This was the Green River, and Ashley here dispatched three parties on beaver-trapping forays, then, with the remaining men, decided to go down the Green by boat. In preparing for this first attempt by Americans to navigate the river, Ashley supervised the building of a thirty-foot bull-boat, then embarked on the unprecedented and dangerous trip. On the first day, while fifteen miles below their starting point, they passed the mouth of a stream that they named the Sandy River, an important crossing point for future travelers on the Oregon Trail. The men found the boat too awkward to manage because it was so heavily loaded. They stopped to build a second boat and set off again.

During the first week, while they enjoyed placid running, they passed Henry's Fork (which enters the Green from the west just north of today's Utah state line in the Ashley National Forest area of the Flaming Gorge National Recreation Area). Ashley decided that here would be the right location for the July rendezvous. He marked it with stakes so that his trappers would easily find it.

"So far the navigation of this river," Ashley wrote, "is without the least obstruction." But then, " . . . we entered between the walls of a range of mountains, which approach at this point to the water's edge on either side of the river and rise almost perpendicular to an immense height. The channel of the river is here contracted to the width of sixty or seventy yards, and the current, much increased in velocity as it rolled along in angry submission to the serpentine walls that direct it, seemed constantly to threaten us with danger as we advanced." (They were in the first of a series of three canyons, the Flaming Gorge, which was to be followed by Horseshoe and Kingfisher Canyons, later named, as were all the other river locations identified below, by Major John Wesley Powell when he made his historic descent of the river in 1869.)

They made camp for the night, and the next day struggled through a dangerous stretch of rapids. Unloading and loading their boats to avoid the worst of the falls and rapids, Ashley came to the Lodore Canyon. Here the river "again enters between two mountains and affords a channel even more contracted than before. As we passed along between these massy walls, which in a great degree excluded from us the rays of heaven and presented a surface as impassable as their body was impregnable, I was forcibly struck with the gloom which spread over the countenances of my men; they seemed to anticipate, and not far distant too, a dreadful termination of our voyage, and I must confess that I partook in some degree of what I supposed to be their feelings, for things around us had truly an awful appearance."

The Bighorn Mountains from the East

Rocks in the rapids caused "a slight injury to our boats," and a mile beyond (at a spot to be named Disaster Falls) the river was too turbulent to navigate. The men unloaded the boats again and anxiously guided them over the falls by means of long ropes. (They were now well into today's Dinosaur National Monument, which lies partly in Utah, partly in Colorado.) There was worse trouble ahead when they passed the mouth of the Yampa River and came to Whirlpool Canyon, "where the mountains again close to the water's edge are in appearance more terrific than any we had seen during the whole voyage. We performed sixteen portages, the most of which were attended with the utmost difficulty and labor." Then, while running the rapids of Split Mountain Canyon, Ashley, who could not swim, came close to disaster when his boat filled with water and almost capsized.

At the Duchesne River (near today's Ouray, Utah) Ashley ended his boat journey on the Green River. He explored Desolation Canyon on foot, and on his return to the river he met a party of the "Eutah [Ute] tribe of Indians, who appeared very glad to see us and treated us in the most respectful and friendly manner. I purchased a few horses and ascended [the Duchesne] to its extreme sources. It was a mountainous sterile country." Ashley then crossed the Uinta Mountains and made his way back to the pre-arranged rendezvous site near the mouth of Henry's Fork of the Green River. At this time, Andrew Henry having decided to retire from the mountains, Ashley made Jedediah Smith a partner in the enterprise.

This was the first rendezvous ever held in the fur trade, an Ashley innovation which revolutionized the business and contributed greatly to his success. Previously, it was accepted practice for fur companies to establish permanent posts—as the British had done in the Northwest, as Astor had planned to do, as Lisa and others, and even Andrew Henry, Ashley's associate, had done—posts from which beaver pelts would be secured largely through trading with the Indians. Ashley wanted to be less dependent on the Indians.

He felt it would be safer, more productive, and more economical to have his men do their own trapping, and to gather annually at a rendezvous where their pelts might be assembled for shipment to St. Louis, and where the trappers might be refurbished for the next year's hunt.

Thanks to his resourcefulness and persistence, Ashley succeeded where others had failed. In October, 1825, he went back to St. Louis with "a hundred or more packs of beaver skin valued at from forty to seventy-five thousand dollars." He repaid his backers, with substantial dividends, and he was on his way to a considerable fortune. In 1826, he made his last trip to the West and sold the fur-trapping end of the business to Jedediah Smith, David Jackson, and William Sublette.

Born in western New York, Jedediah Smith was twenty-three in 1822, when he "came down to St. Louis and hearing of an expedition that was fitting out for the prosecution of the fur trade on the head of the Missouri, by Gen. Wm. H. Ashley and Major Henry, I called on Gen. Ashley to make an engagement to go with him as a hunter. I found no difficulty in making a bargain on as good terms as I had reason to expect."

Smith described the trip up the Missouri on Henry and Ashley's first expedition as "slow, laborious and dangerous." When the expedition reached the Yellowstone he was assigned to a party dispatched to the Musselshell River. Winter began to set in, and the party built a sturdy house for an encampment. "When the weather had at length become extremely cold and the ice strong and firm across the river, we were astonished to see the buffalo come

THE WIND RIVER RANGE, WYOMING

95

pouring from all sides into the valley of the Missouri, and particularly the vast bands that came from the north and crossed over to the south side on the ice. We therefore had them in thousands around us and nothing more required of us than to select and kill the best for our use whenever we might choose."

After his winter sojourn on the Musselshell, Smith was dispatched by Henry to join Ashley's second expedition and to ask him to secure replacement horses. James Clyman, a surveyor, was the Ashley expedition's clerk and a member of the party of eleven dispatched under Jedediah Smith's command to rejoin the trappers at Henry's post.

It was on this journey that Jedediah Smith, as well as surviving an Indian attack, suffered the first terrible accident of his career, as described by Clyman in memoirs written years later.

"A large grssley came down the valley and struck us. Capt Smith being in the advance he and the bear met face to face. Grissly did not hesitate a moment but sprung on the capt taking him by the head first breaking several of his ribs and cutting his head badly.

"None of us having any sugical knowledge what was to be done—I asked the capt what was best. He said one or two go for water and if you have a needle and thread git it out and sew up my wounds around my head which was bleeding freely. I got a pair of scissors and cut off his har and then began my first job of dressing wounds. Upon examination I found the bear had taken nearly all his head in his capacious mouth close to his left eye on one side and close to his right ear on the other, and laid the skull bare to near the corner of the head leaving a white streak whare his teeth passed. One of his ears was torn from his head out to the outer rim.

"After stitching all the wounds in the best way I was capabl and according to the captains directions the ear being the last I told him I could do nothing for his ear. O you must try to stitch up some way or other he said. Then I put in my needle stitching it through and through and over and over laying the lacerated parts together as nice as I could with my hands. Water was found and the captain was able to mount his horse and ride to camp where we pitched a tent the onley one we had and made him as comfortable as circumstances would permit. This gave us a lesson on the character of the grissly bear which we did not forget."

Smith made a remarkable recovery from his severe wounds and Clyman's crude surgery, and he was able in less than a fortnight to reassume command. He led the party beyond the Black Hills (into Wyoming), on to the Powder River." ...stoping and traping for beaver occasionly crossing several steep and high ridges which in any other country would be called mountains." (They were the southern foothills of the Bighorn Mountains.)

When the men arrived at Wind River, which Clyman thought was "well named," in that "strong north winds prevailed continually." Smith led them along the eastern side of the mountain slopes "untill we came immediately north of Freemont Peak on the Wind River

Mountain whare we halted for the winter." (The peak was named for John Frémont many years later.) After several weeks among the Crows, Smith took his party southward to the Sweetwater River, and in February 1824 an event of singular importance in the opening of the West occurred. At the time Clyman was unaware of its significance, and reported only that "we found we had crossed the main ridge of the Rocky mountan."

Jedediah Smith, William Sublette, Thomas Fitzpatrick, James Clyman, and the other members of the party had discovered the heart of the South Pass across the Rocky Mountains. Robert Stuart and his party of Astorians had come through the mountains on their eastbound journey somewhat to the south of the section where Smith and his men had crossed the pass westbound. Smith would make many more notable explorations in the West, but none would be more commercially important than the establishment of the South Pass, the gateway through the Rockies on the Oregon Trail. The discovery of the central pass paved the way for the use of wagons in the mountain fur trade by William Ashley, William Sublette, and Benjamin Bonneville, and this, in turn, paved the way for future emigrant wagon-trains.

Jedediah Smith now turned his efforts to new horizons, deciding to trap the area northwest of the Green River, in territory dominated by the British fur trade, although by the joint-occupation agreement it was also legal territory of the United States.

Smith's expedition into Oregon Country was to have enormous significance, presaging the breakup of British dominance. The abundance of beaver, which would be reported by Smith, would attract other trappers. The beauty and rich potential of the Northwest, reported by them as well as by Smith, would attract emigrants. And missionaries. And more settlers. The British, who saw the Northwest only as a source for the fur trade, would witness with discomfort the ever-increasing American occupation. The new settlers' appeals to the federal government for a more positive stand against the British would be a strong influence in bringing about an abrogation of the joint-occupation agreement.

At the rendezvous of Ashley's forces in April 1825, Smith found Clyman, as well as Thomas Fitzpatrick, alive. It was there that Ashley made Smith a partner in his enterprise. After the rendezvous he accompanied Ashley, and the valuable pelts, to St. Louis.

In November 1825, Smith headed back to the mountains, leading an expedition to Cache Valley, Utah. Then in the spring of 1826, he led a party to the Great Salt Lake, where, from Promontory Point, he dispatched four men in a bull-boat—James Clyman, Henry Fraeb, Moses Harris, and Louis Vasquez—to make a historic first reconnoiter of the mysterious lake. The men explored the western shoreline for twenty-four days before returning to camp.

After the 1826 summer rendezvous in Cache Valley, when Ashley sold out to Smith, Sublette, and Jackson, Smith assumed responsibility for trapping beaver in virgin territory west of Utah. He led a party of fifteen on an expedition that was to be the greatest of his career and the most significant since those of Lewis and Clark and Zebulon Pike.

Jedediah Smith 1826-28

··············· 1827

Quoted material in this chapter is from the journal of Jedediah Strong Smith as well as a letter he wrote to Meriwether Lewis. Material has also been taken from the journal of Harrison Rogers.

Chapter 8

JEDEDIAH STRONG SMITH: ACROSS THE DESERT TO CALIFORNIA

The mountain men who had been assembled by William Ashley had, in their first three years of trapping and exploring, opened a vast central portion of the West beyond the Rockies. In the summer of 1826, Jedediah Smith and his party traveled farther west than any Americans other than the Lewis and Clark expedition. The Great Captains had crossed the northwest wilderness to Oregon Country; Jedediah Smith would cross the southwest wilderness to California.

He wrote in a letter to Clark: "My general course on leaving the Salt Lake was SW and W. Passing the little Uta Lake [Utah Lake] and ascending Ashley's river [the Sevier River]. I passed over a range of mountains running SE and NW and struck a river running SW which I called Adams River, in compliment to our President." (The river is the Virgin, which descends to the Colorado west of the Grand Canyon.)

He followed the Virgin past today's Zion National Park. When he came to the Colorado he crossed it at what is now Lake Mead, created by Hoover Dam, entering today's Arizona, and followed its eastern banks to the beautiful Mojave Valley. He then " ... travelled a west course fifteen days over a country of complete barrens generally travelling from morning until night without water. I crossed a Salt plain about 20 miles long and 8 wide; on the surface was a crust of beautiful white salt, quite thin. Under this surface there is a layer of salt from a half to one and a half inches in depth; between this and the upper layer there is about four inches of yellowish sand."

Smith and his party arrived in the province of the Upper California via the San Bernardino Mountains and Cajon Pass, but were denied permission to hunt and sent back the way they came. But after he and his party crossed the San Bernardino Mountains, Smith veered northward from his original route, crossed the Santa Clara River, and continued north to Tulare Lake and north again to the Stanislaus River.

Here, Smith writes, he "made a small hunt and attempted to take my party across [the mountains]." In early spring deep snow made the crossing of the Sierra Nevadas impossible. In the failed attempt five horses starved to death, and Smith had to return to the valley until late spring when he, with two companions, made the difficult crossing. Leaving the rest of his party to trap in the Stanislaus vicinity, Smith's detachment of three trekked into Nevada, proceeded south of Walker Lake, then across the desert to Ely, Nevada.

WALKER LAKE, NEVADA

"After travelling twenty days from the east side of Mount Joseph [the Sierra Mountains], I struck the SW corner of the Great Salt Lake, travelling over a country completely barren and destitute of game. We frequently travelled without water sometimes for two days over sandy deserts, where there was no sign of vegetation...When we arrived at the Salt Lake, we had but one horse and one mule remaining."

Despite the rigorous trip he had just completed, Smith was ready to set off again after only ten days' rest. This time he headed west to rejoin the group of trappers he had left on the Stanislaus River in California, where he expected to find beaver but confessed, "I was also led on by the love of novelty common to all, which is much increased by the pursuit of its gratification."

He chose to take the more circuitous route to the Colorado with his eighteen men, moved beyond the Great Salt Lake, and found an easier pass over the Wasatch Range. When he reached the Colorado River he paused to trade with Mojave Indians who attacked Smith's men as they, having put aside their arms, were starting to cross the river. Ten men were killed, but Smith and the rest of the party reached a sand bar in the river. "I was yet on the sand bar in sight of my dead companions and not far off were hundreds of Indians who might in all probability close in upon us. Such articles as would sink I threw in the river and spread the rest out on the sand bar. I told the men what kind of Country we had to pass through and gave them permission to take such things as they chose from the bar."

Smith then scattered the rest of the goods over the ground, "knowing that whilst the indians were quarrelling over the division of the spoils we would be gaining time for our escape. We then moved on in the almost hopeless endeavor to travel over the desert Plain where there was not the least possibility of finding game for our subsistence."

Smith's party trudged into the desert. Fighting thirst, hunger, heat, and exhaustion, they arrived in California, Smith again crossing the San Bernardino Mountains by way of Cajon Pass. He then moved up to the Stanislaus River to rejoin the trappers he had left there in the spring. He "found them all well. They had passed a pleasant summer, not in the least interrupted by the indians, and they spoke in high terms of the climate."

Smith then rode to the San Jose Mission, where he was detained for several days, sent under guard to Monterey, and told to leave California. He retrieved his men from the Stanislaus and at year-end headed north. "Having been so long absent from the business of trapping, and so much perplexed and harassed by the folly of men in power, I returned again to the woods, the river, the prairie, the camp and the game with a feeling somewhat like that of a prisoner escaped from his dungeon and his chains."

During the spring of 1828, Smith's party worked its way northward, trapping beaver along the San Joaquin River and its tributaries, and along the American River. The party then crossed the Sacramento River and entered the labyrinthine terrain of today's Trinity National Forest, east of Eureka. Ravines and rocks took their toll on the men and the horses. "Two of my horses were dashed in pieces from the precipices and many others terribly mangled." Dense coastal fogs obscured the trails, some of which, even in late April, were covered with snow up to four feet deep.

After much suffering in the attempt to follow the Trinity and the Klamath rivers, the party heard that "the Ocean was not more than 15 or 18 miles distant," from two men who had been sent ahead to scout. Ten days later, on June 8, Smith was finally able to note in his journal that the party "encamped on the shore of the Ocean" (near Requa).

On June 19, Smith followed an Indian trail northward and "struck a river 80 yards wide." He was a few miles south of the 42nd parallel, and the river, which he crossed a few days later, now bears his name. By early July, after crossing the Rogue River, the party reached the Coquille River.

He then led the party on to the Umpqua River, where they had a run-in with Indians who called themselves Kelawatsets. On July 14, seventeen of Smith's party were killed.

Smith and two companions who had been out scouting escaped, finding their way to a Hudson's Bay Company post, Fort Vancouver, located a hundred miles to the north.

Smith remained with the British traders until March 12, 1829, "when he ascended the Columbia and passed several trading posts until he came to the Kettle Falls, Fort Colville; from there he proceeded on, passing the Flathead trading post on the Flathead River, until he joined one [of] his partners [David Jackson] in the Kootenais country; from there he proceeded and joined Mr. W. L. Sublette on the 5th August 1829, at the Tetons on Henry's Fork S. Branch Columbia."

After two more trapping parties, Smith had had enough of the mountains, and at the Wind River rendezvous in 1830, he and his partners sold their firm to Thomas Fitzpatrick, Milton Sublette, James Bridger, Henry Fraeb, and Jean Baptiste Gervais, who went on to operate as the Rocky Mountain Fur Company. Smith returned to St. Louis, bought a farm and a house, and planned to work on a comprehensive journal of his travels, along with a map of the country he had come to know so well. But before settling down, he determined to try his hand at a trading trip to Santa Fe, one motive for which may have been his desire to learn more about the Southwest, for inclusion in the book he hoped to write.

On April 10, 1831, the caravan departed from St. Louis, led by Jedediah Smith, William Sublette, and David Jackson. Thomas Fitzpatrick joined his former comrades at Independence. When the caravan reached the trackless, arid Cimarron Cut-off, a late-spring drought threatened disaster for the more than seventy caravan members, and Jedediah Smith set off alone to find water. He never returned, and his companions learned later that he had been slain by Comanches.

As historian Hiram Chittenden put it, "A sadder fate or a more heroic victim the parched wastes of the desert never knew."

As a result of his experiences, Josiah Gregg wrote a book that is regarded as the most authoritative source of the history of the Santa Fe trade and life on the early Santa Fe Trail: Commerce of the Prairies; the Journal of a Santa Fe Trader. *It is from this classic trailblazer chronicle that the narrative material in this chapter has been extracted.*

Chapter 9

JOSIAH GREGG: ON THE SANTA FE TRAIL

On May 27, 1831, the day Jedediah Smith was searching for water near the end of the Santa Fe Trail on the Cimarron Cut-off, Josiah Gregg, whose father had been a member of William Becknell's 1822 expedition to Santa Fe, was near the start of the trail in Council Grove, on the first of his many trips to New Mexico. It was ten years since Mexico had declared independence, the Santa Fe trade was flourishing, the trail had been surveyed, and a treaty had been signed with the Indians. But, at the time of Gregg's first trip, the trail to Santa Fe was still unprotected and the Indians still dangerous.

Illness had prevented Gregg from pursuing his medical practice in Missouri. He was advised "to take a trip across the prairies" and joined one of the annual spring caravans from the United States to Santa Fe. The caravan "consisted of nearly a hundred wagons—about half drawn by ox-teams, the rest by mules—besides a dozen of dearborns and other small vehicles and two small cannons, each mounted upon a carriage."

The route "lay through an uninterrupted prairie for about fifty miles—in fact, I may say, for five hundred miles, excepting the very narrow fringes of timber along the borders of the streams." On the third day of travel, "our eyes were greeted with the sight of a herd of buffalo quietly grazing in the distance before us. The excitement that the first sight of these prairie beeves occasions among a party of novices beggars all description. A few beeves were killed during the chase and the savory viands eaten with a relish rarely experienced at the well-spread tables of the most fashionable and wealthy."

The caravan reached the Arkansas River several miles to the east of its great bend, "the majestic river averaging at least a quarter of a mile in width, bespeckled with verdant islets, thickly set with cottonwood timber." Twenty miles beyond, "the attention of the traveler is directed to the Pawnee Rock upon whose surface are furrowed, in uncouth but legible characters, numerous dates and the names of various travelers who have chanced to pass that way." (Like Independence Rock on the Oregon Trail, Pawnee Rock was an important landmark for travelers; it gradually eroded through the years and has largely vanished.)

A PRAIRIE DOG

By mid-June "our route had led up the course of the Arkansas River for over a hundred miles." (The average distance traveled daily by a caravan was fifteen miles; Gregg's was traveling more slowly.) A regular ford had never been established on the Arkansas. "Nor was there a road, not even a trail, anywhere across the famous plain extending between the Arkansas and Cimarron rivers, a distance of over fifty miles [the Cimarron Cut-off] which now lay before us—the scene of such frequent sufferings in former times for want of water. It having been determined upon, however, to strike across this dreaded desert the following morning, the whole party was busy in preparing for the water scrape, as these droughty drives are appropriately called by previous travelers."

The caravan, with its wagons extended for more than a mile, headed onto the desert. Approaching the valley of the Cimarron "we discovered a countless host [of Indians] pouring over the opposite ridge, and galloping directly towards us." The wagons moved quickly into defensive positions, and the men readied their rifles. "The Indians were collecting around us, however, in such great numbers that it was deemed expedient to force them away so as to resume our march, or at least to take a more advantageous position.

"Our company was therefore mustered and drawn up in line of battle; and accompanied by a sound of drum and fife we marched towards the main group of Indians. The latter seemed far more delighted than frightened with this strange parade and music, a spectacle they had no doubt never witnessed before, and perhaps looked upon the whole movement rather as a complimentary salute than a hostile array." The principal chief approached Captain Stanley "smoking the pipe of peace."

The traders entered New Mexico slightly to the northeast of today's Kiowa National Grasslands on the Oklahoma border. "The wildness of this place, with its towering cliffs, craggy spurs, and deep-cut crevices, became doubly impressive to us as we reflected that we were in the very midst of savage haunts. Often will the lonely traveler as he plods his weary way in silence imagine in each click of a pebble the snap of a firelock, and in every rebound of a twig the whish of an arrow."

At Rabbit-Ear Mountain (near Clayton), a landmark for travelers on the trail, there appeared a "Mexican 'cibolero,' or 'buffalo-hunter'" who announced "a piece of most melancholy news—the tragical death of a celebrated mountain adventurer" who had been slain by Indians somewhere along the Cimarron. The slain man was Jedediah Strong Smith.

Gregg recounts the story of Smith's lone search for water for his party of twenty wagons and some eighty men, and concludes:

"He had already wandered many miles away from his comrades when, on turning over an eminence, his eyes were joyfully greeted with the appearance of a small stream meandering through the valley that spread before him. It was the Cimarron. He hurried forward to slake the fire of his parched lips, but imagine his disappointment at finding in the channel only a bed of dry sand. While with his head bent down [to dig for water], in the effort to quench his burning thirst in the fountain, he was pierced by the arrows of a gang of Comanches who were lying in wait for him! Yet he struggled bravely to the last; and, as the Indians themselves have since related, killed two or three of their party before he was overpowered. The companions of Capt. Smith, having descended upon the Cimarron at another point, appear to have remained ignorant of the terrible fate that had befallen him until they were informed of the circumstances by some Mexican traders . . ."

The lesson taught by this tragic tale to Gregg and the other traders who had been traveling not far behind the Smith and Sublette party, and had survived encounters with Indians on the trail, was never to wander away from the safety of a caravan.

Continuing along the Cimarron Cut-off of the Santa Fe Trail (on what is now Interstate Highway 25), the traders came to the Canadian River (near Springer, New Mexico). Gregg noted that this major nine-hundred-mile-long river of the Southwest "is here but a rippling brook hardly a dozen paces in width, though eighty miles from its source in the mountains to the north. The stream is called Rio Colorado by the Mexicans [and the Indians], and is known among Americans by its literal translation of Red River." (Major Long, on his 1820 expedition, mistook the Canadian River for the Red River on hearing the Indians term it the "Colorado.")

Here the caravan was met by "a dozen or more of our countrymen from Taos—sixty or seventy miles distant—to which town there is a direct but rugged route across the mountains" (Taos Trail).

After having been met by Mexican "escorts," the traders proceeded in detached, unorganized ranks, "at last out of danger of Indian hostilities, although still nearly a hundred and forty miles from Santa Fe." The trail stretched along the east of the Sangre de Cristo Mountains to San Miguel. From this "first settlement of any note upon our route," consisting of "irregular clusters of mud-walled huts," the trail "makes a great southern bend to find a passway through the broken extremity of the spur of mountains," and ascends to Santa Fe.

"'Oh, we are approaching the suburbs!' thought I, on perceiving cornfields and what I supposed to be brick-kilns scattered in every direction. A friend at my elbow said, 'It is true those are heaps of unburnt brick, nevertheless they are houses—this is the city of Santa Fe!'

"The arrival produced a great deal of bustle and excitement among the natives. 'Los Americanos! Los carros! La entrada de caravana!' were to be heard in every direction; and crowds of women and boys flocked around to see the new-comers; while crowds of 'leperos' hung about to see what they could pilfer.

"The wagoners were by no means free from excitement on the occasion; they had spent the morning in rubbing up, and now they were prepared, with clean faces, sleek-combed hair, and their choicest Sunday suits to meet the fair eyes of glistening black that were sure to stare at them as they passed. There was yet another preparation to be made in order to show off to advantage. Each wagoner must tie a brand new cracker to the lash of his whip; for on driving through the streets and the 'plaza publica' every one strives to outvie his comrades in the dexterity with which he flourishes this favorite badge of his authority."

So, at the end of the Santa Fe Trail, arduous and dangerous though the trek may have been, there was excitement and entertainment in the exotic society that greeted the traders, and big profits to be made. It would be many years before pleasures comparable to those that greeted traders in Santa Fe would await those who chose to follow the Oregon Trail.

Washington Irving's introduction to Captain Bonneville had been arranged by John Jacob Astor, the sponsor of Irving's earlier book about the pioneering explorations of the fur-trading Astorians. Irving titled his new work The Rocky Mountains, or Scenes, Incidents and Adventures in the Far West; Digested from the Journal of Captain B. L. E. Bonneville of the Army of the United States, and Illustrated from Various Other Sources. *He wrote that "the work is substantially the narrative of the worthy captain, and many of its most graphic passages are but little varied from his own language."*

Chapter 10

BENJAMIN BONNEVILLE: ON THE OREGON TRAIL

Captain Benjamin Louis Eulalie de Bonneville entered the western scene in May of 1832. Major trails to the West had been blazed, but emigration had not begun. Thanks to Captain Bonneville—and Nathaniel Wyeth, who headed west the same year—Americans would soon begin to settle the West.

French-born and well-connected, Bonneville, a graduate of West Point, headed an expedition financed largely by Alfred Seton of New York, an associate of John Jacob Astor and member of the Astorian party two decades earlier. Bonneville was also instructed by the War Department to gather intelligence concerning the war-making capabilities of the western Indians, as well as a wide range of information about the West, an assignment reflecting the incipient American expansionist interest. It was Bonneville who, during his expedition, demonstrated that the as yet unnamed Oregon Trail could be traversed by wagons all the way from the Missouri River to the Green River via the recently discovered South Pass.

The party of 110 men, "most of whom were experienced hunters and trappers," departed for the West on May 1, 1832, from Fort Osage on the Missouri River, using wagons instead of mules and pack-horses. "Though he was to travel through a trackless wilderness, yet the greater part of his route would lie across open plains destitute of forest, and where wheel carriages can pass in every direction. The chief difficulty would be in passing the deep ravines cut through the prairies by streams and winter torrents. Here it would be often necessary to dig a road down the banks, and to make bridges for the [twenty] wagons."

·-------- Bonneville, 1832-34

The caravan followed what was to become the Oregon Trail from the Kansas River to the Platte, and along the North Platte. Following the North Platte into Wyoming, Captain Bonneville "had been made sensible of the great elevation of country which he was gradually ascending, by the effect of the dryness and rarefaction of the atmosphere upon his wagons. The woodwork shrunk; the paint boxes of the wheels were continually working out, and it was necessary to support the spokes by stout props to prevent their falling asunder." When the caravan entered the Laramie Mountains (Medicine Bow National Forest) "their journey became irksome in the extreme. Rugged steeps and deep ravines incessantly obstructed their progress, so that a great part of the day was spent in the painful toil of digging through banks, filling up ravines, forcing the wagons up the most forbidding ascents, or swinging them with ropes down the face of dangerous precipices."

On July 24, a historic event occurred. "The travellers took final leave of the Sweet water, and keeping westwardly, over a low and very rocky ridge, one of the most southern spurs of the Wind River Mountains [South Pass] they encamped, after a march of seven hours and a half, on the banks of a small clear stream [the Little Sandy River] running to the south. Captain Bonneville now considered himself as having fairly passed the crest of the Rocky Mountains; and felt some degree of exultation in being the first individual that had crossed, north of the settled provinces of Mexico, from the waters of the Atlantic to those of the Pacific, with the wagons."

Captain Bonneville then moved his party up the Green River to a point near the mouth of the Horse Creek (Daniel, Wyoming), where he built a log fort which he occupied for only a short time before moving on toward the headwaters of the Salmon River in Idaho.

"The nature of the country through which he was about to travel rendered it impossible to proceed with wagons. He had more goods and supplies of various kinds, also, than were required for present purposes, or than could be conveniently transported on horseback; aided, therefore, by a few confidential men, he made caches, or secret pits, during the night, when the rest of the camp were asleep, and in this deposited the superfluous effects, together with the wagons." The route to Salmon River "lay up the valley of the Seeds-kee-dee [Indian name for the Green River], overlooked to the right by the lofty peaks of the Wind River Mountains. From bright little lakes and fountain-heads of this remarkable bed of mountains poured forth the tributary streams. So transparent were these waters that the trout with which they abounded could be seen gliding about as if in the air; and their pebbly beds were distinctly visible at the depth of many feet. This beautiful and diaphanous quality of the Rocky Mountain streams prevails for a long time after they have mingled their waters and swollen into important rivers."

From Jackson Hole, Bonneville crossed into Idaho via Teton Pass to Pierre's Hole (Teton Basin) and, when he reached the upper waters of the Salmon River, stopped to establish winter quarters a few miles below the mouth of the Lemhi River. In his post on the Salmon River, Captain Bonneville "was now in the full enjoyment of his wishes; leading a hunter's life in the heart of the wilderness, with all its wild populace around him. Besides his own people, motley in character and costume—Creole, Kentuckian, Indian, half-breed, hired trapper, and

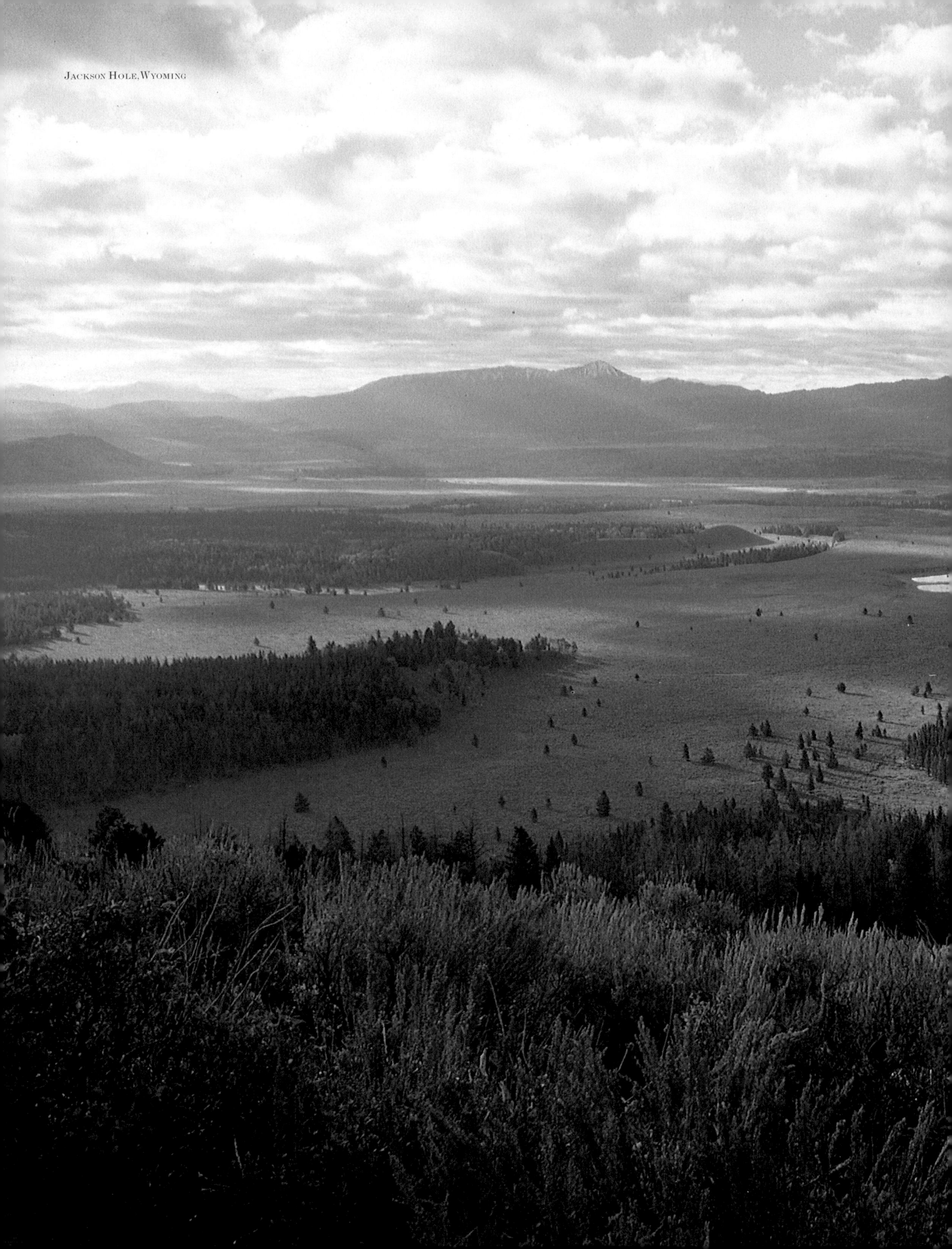
Jackson Hole, Wyoming

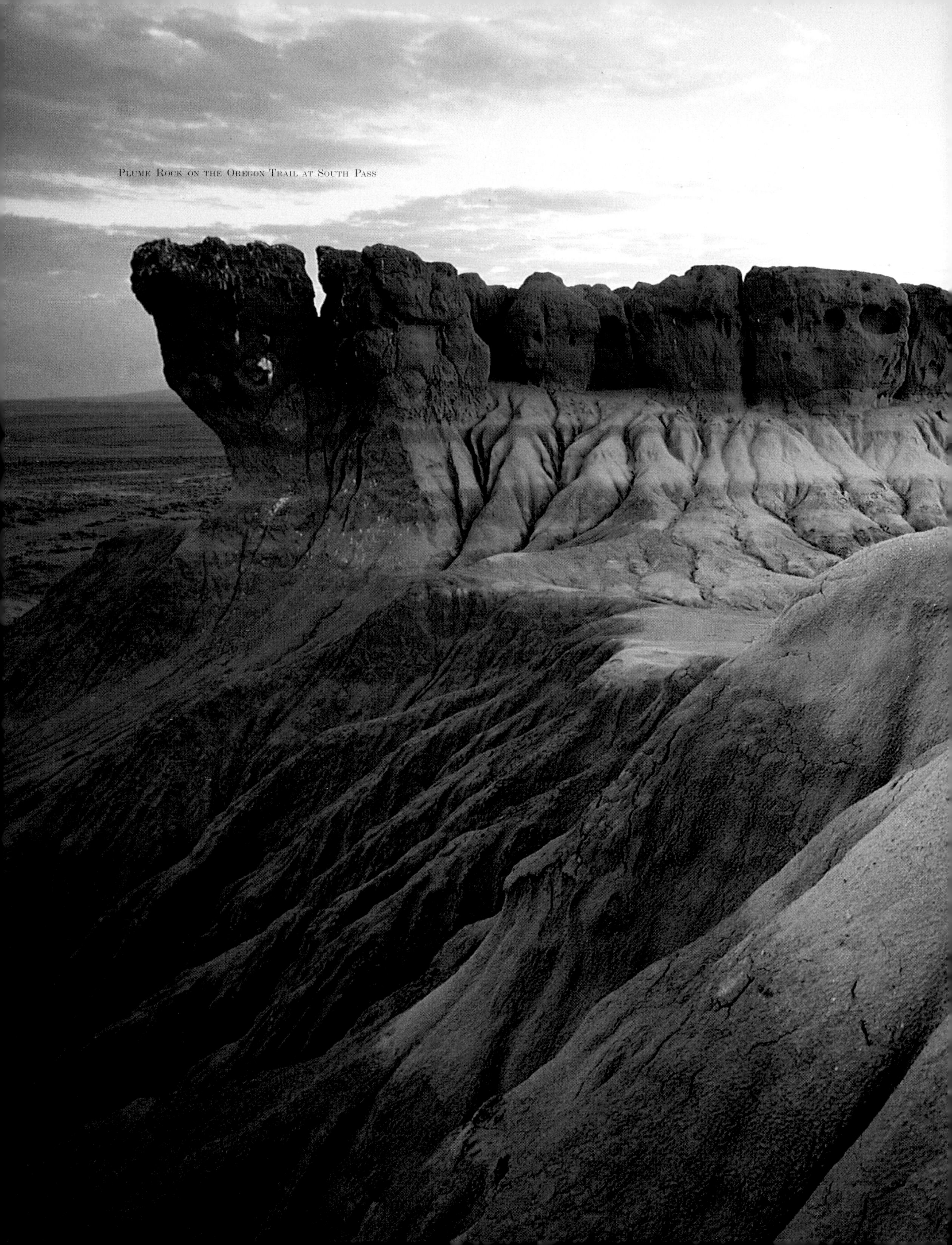

Plume Rock on the Oregon Trail at South Pass

ON THE OREGON TRAIL

free trapper—he was surrounded by encampments of Nez Perces and Flatheads, with their droves of horses covering the hills and plains."

Soon, however, Bonneville had to leave his wilderness paradise, for lack of food and supplies. "He detached fifty men [led by Joseph Walker] toward the south to winter upon the Snake River, and to trap its waters in the spring, with orders to rejoin him in the month of July at Horse Creek in Green River Valley [near Fort Bonneville]." He himself, with a small number of trappers, joined his new friends, the Nez Perces and Flatheads, and "adapted the Indian mode of moving with the game and grass." The Indians led Bonneville to winter quarters on the Lemhi River "in a natural fortress of the mountains."

In the spring of 1833, Bonneville, finding his chosen territory for the season's beaver hunt taken by the Rocky Mountain Fur Company, decided to "carry his expedition into some of the unknown tracts of the Far West, beyond what is generally termed the buffalo range," and "to establish a trading post on the lower part of the Columbia River, near the Multnomah Valley [the Willamette] and to endeavor to retrieve for his country some of the lost trade of Astoria." He also determined to "have the Great Salt Lake properly explored, and all its secrets revealed," a project which he assigned to his lieutenant, Joseph Walker.

Before heading for the Columbia, Bonneville led his party to the Bighorn River, traveling again through South Pass to the Wind River, and finally established winter camp near the Portneuf River (vicinity of Pocatello, Idaho).

He "next prepared for a reconnoitering expedition of great extent and peril—to penetrate to the Hudson's Bay establishments on the banks of the Columbia ... This expedition would,

of course, take him through the Snake River country and across the Blue Mountains, the scenes of so much hardship and disaster to Hunt and Crooks and their Astorian bands . . . and he would have to pass through it in the same frightful season, the depth of winter."

When he reached the Powder River at its confluence with the Snake in Oregon, Bonneville came upon large numbers of the Shoshone branch of Snake Indians, dubbed "Diggers" by the trappers, "from their subsisting in great measure on the roots of the earth . . . Their greatest passion was for a mirror. It was a 'great medicine' in their eyes. The sight of one was sufficient at any time to throw them into a paroxysm of eagerness and delight, and they were ready to give anything they had for the smallest fragment in which they might behold their . . . features."

By March 1834, after an extremely trying trip over the Blue Mountains, Bonneville and three companions arrived at Fort Walla Walla of the Hudson's Bay Company, on the Columbia River (a trading post built in 1818, and first named Fort Nez Perce, by Donald McKenzie, the former Astorian).

Bonneville "set off as soon as possible" to return to the Portneuf encampment. He planned "soon to return with a stronger party, more completely fitted to the purpose."

The Blue Mountains proved even more difficult than they had been on the trek westward. Bonneville came to a long pass "so heavily piled with snow that it seemed impracticable." But he devised an ingenious plan. "This was to make two light sleds, place the packs on them, and drag them to the other side of the mountain, thus forming a road in the wet snow which, should it afterward freeze, would be sufficiently hard to bear the horses. The sleds were constructed, the heavy baggage was drawn backward and forward until the road was beaten, when they desisted from their fatiguing labors. The night turned out clear and cold, and by morning the road was encrusted with ice sufficiently strong for their purpose. They now set out on their icy turnpike and got on well enough, excepting that now and then a horse would slide out of the track and immediately sink up to the neck. Then came on toil and difficulty, and they would be obliged to haul up the floundering animal with ropes. One, more unlucky than the rest, after repeated falls had to be abandoned in the snow. Notwithstanding these repeated delays they succeeded, before the sun had acquired sufficient power to thaw the snow, in getting all the rest of their horses safely to the other side of the mountain."

When at length he was reunited with his main party on the Bear River, northeast of the Great Salt Lake, he learned of the failure of Joseph Walker's expedition, assigned to find beaver further west. "The Great Salt Lake still remained unexplored; at the same time, the means which had been furnished so liberally to fit out this favorite expedition, had all been squandered at Monterey; and the peltries, also, which had been collected along the way."

In concluding the Bonneville story, Washington Irving wrote: "We here close our picturings of the Rocky Mountains and their wild inhabitants, and of the wild life that prevails there. We are aware that this singular state of things is full of mutation and must soon undergo great changes, if not entirely pass away. The fur trade itself, which has given life to all this

portraiture, is essentially evanescent. Rival parties of trappers soon exhaust the streams, especially when competition renders them heedless and wasteful of the beaver. The fur-bearing animals extinct, a complete change will come over the scene; the gay fur trapper and his steed, decked out in wild array and tinkling with bells and trinketry; the savage war chief, plumed and painted and ever on the prowl; the traders' cavalcade, winding through defiles or ever naked plains with the stealthy war party lurking on its trail; the buffalo chase, the hunting camp, the mad carouse in the midst of danger, the night attack, the stampede, the scamper, the fierce skirmish among rocks and cliffs, all this romance of savage life, which yet exists [1838] among the mountains will then exist but in frontier story, and seem like the fictions of chivalry or fairy tale."

THE POWDER RIVER VALLEY, OREGON

Quoted material for this chapter was taken from the Narrative of the Adventures of Zenas Leonard, Written by Himself.

Chapter 11

ZENAS LEONARD:
JOSEPH WALKER BLAZES A TRAIL TO NORTHERN CALIFORNIA

What Captain Benjamin Bonneville regarded as the failed expedition of Joseph Reddeford Walker, was in reality one of the greatest feats of Western exploration. Instead of castigating Walker, the captain should have praised and rewarded him, for it was Walker's achievements that were ultimately recognized as the most enduring of Bonneville's contributions to America's opening of the Far West.

Washington Irving described Walker as a "native of Tennessee, about six feet high, strong built, dark complexioned, brave in spirit though mild in manners. He had resided for many years in Missouri, on the frontier, had been among the earliest adventurers to Santa Fe where he went [with William Becknell] to trap beaver."

Zenas Leonard, a young Pennsylvanian in the mountains as a free trapper for about two years, joined the Bonneville party and was assigned to Walker's brigade, "which was ordered to steer through an unknown country towards the Pacific, and if he did not find beaver, he should return to the Great Salt Lake in the following summer. Mr. Walker was a man well calculated to undertake a business of this kind. He was well hardened to the hardships of the wilderness, understood the character of the Indians very well, was kind and affable to his men, but at the same time at liberty to command without giving offence, and to explore unknown regions was his delight."

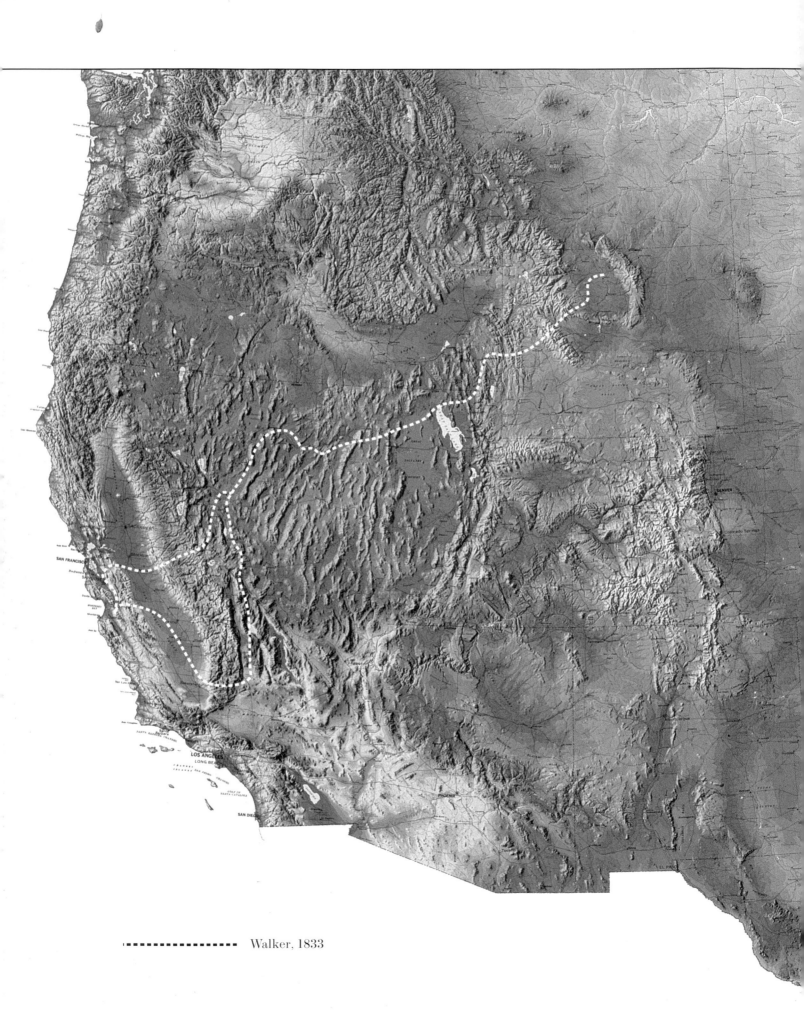

•••••••••••••••••••••• Walker, 1833

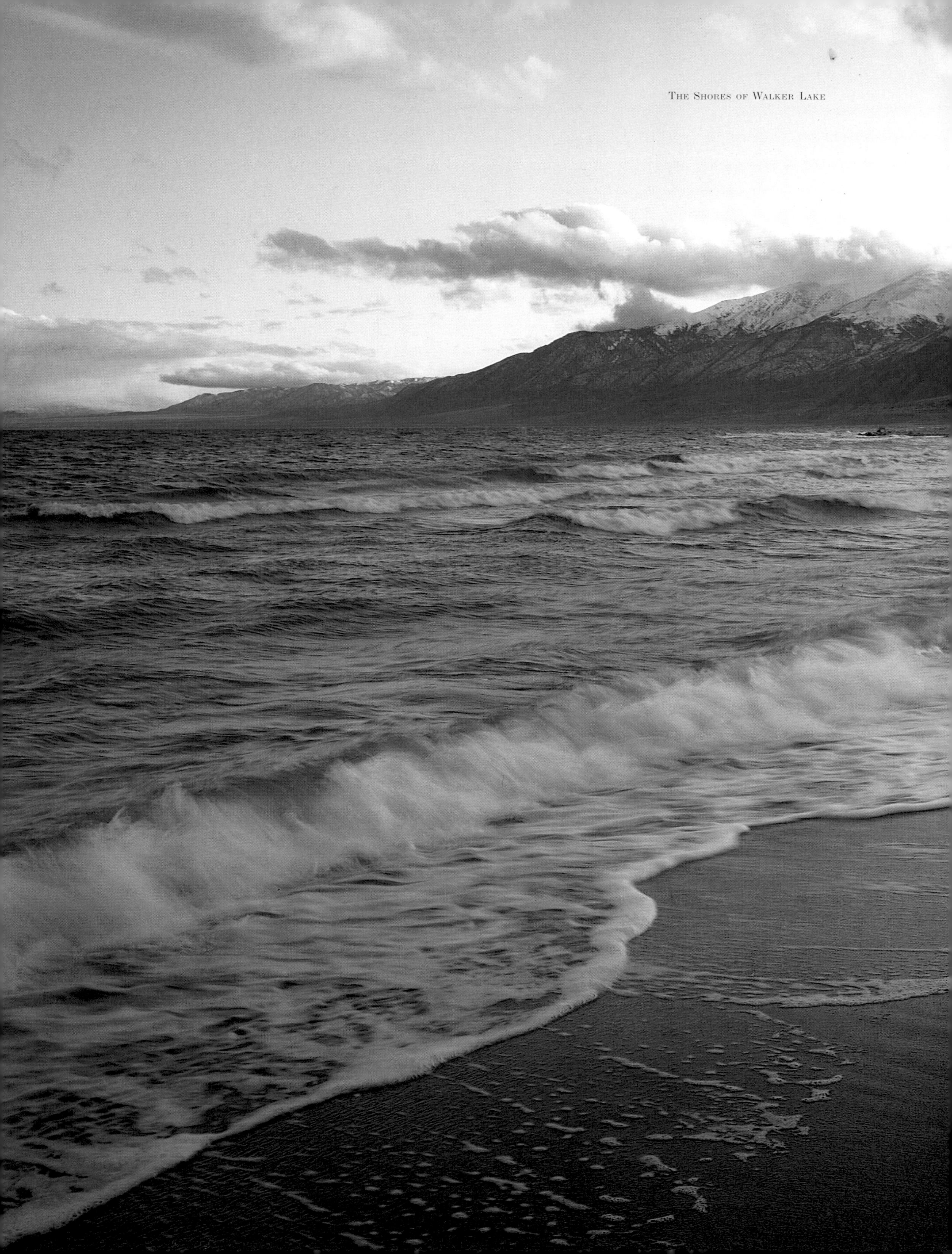

The Shores of Walker Lake

The Walker expedition set off on July 24, 1833. "We continued along the margin of the [Great Salt] Lake with the intention of leaving it when we got to the extreme west side of it." Beyond the lake they "took a westerly course into the most extensive and barren plains I have ever seen."

In the unexplored wasteland of the Great Salt Lake desert they met a band of Indians whose chief told them "that after travelling so many days southwest, the course we were now about to take [north of Jedediah Smith's desert treks], we would come to a high mountain [Pilot Peak on the Nevada border] and on each side of which we would find a large river to head and descend into the sandy plains below, forming innumerable small lakes, and sinks into the earth and disappears [Humboldt River]." The chief also warned them that they "would come across a tribe of poor Indians [Diggers] whom he supposed would not be friendly."

In the relentless desert the men "began to show symptoms of fatigue, the terrain having become so dry and sandy that there is scarcely any vegetation to be found, not even a spear of grass except around the springs. The water in some of these springs, too, is so salt that it is impossible to drink it." When they reached the Humboldt River they began to come across Digger Indians. At the hut of one of the Diggers "we obtained a large robe composed of beaver skins fastened together, in exchange for two awls and a fish hook. This robe was worth from 30 to 40 dollars."

Though there was little beaver to be found in the Humboldt, their traps were much coveted by the Indians. Captain Walker, learning belatedly that some of his men had killed Indians they had found stealing the traps, "immediately took measures for its effectual suppression."

THE HUMBOLDT RIVER SINK

After leaving the Humboldt Sinks, which the trappers named Battle Lakes, the party crossed the river on rafts built of tule bulrushes, went on to an encampment on Carson Sink, and from there to the lake which later bore Walker's name in western Nevada. The Sierra Nevada Mountains now loomed ahead, and (from today's Bridgeport, California) "we sent out several scouting parties to search out a pass over the mountains." One of the scouting parties "had found an Indian path which they thought led over the mountain [and] in the morning we started on our toilsome journey. Ascending the mountain we found to be very difficult from the rocks and its steepness. In taking a view the next morning of the extensive plains through which we had travelled, its appearance is awfully sublime [the Great Basin of Nevada]. As far as the eye can reach, you can see nothing but an unbroken level, tiresome to the eye to behold. The sight [eastward] meets with nothing but a poor sandy plain, extending from the base of the Rocky Mountains to the level below, interspersed with several rivers winding their way, here and there forming innumerable lakes having their margins thinly adorned with a few withering and fading cottonwood trees where the water ceases to flow and sinks into the sand."

The crossing of the Sierra Nevada was one of the most difficult treks in the annals of Western exploration. The horses "began to grow stupid and stiff, and we began to despair of getting them over the mountain"; they bogged down in snow drifts and were pulled out by the men, who by then were exhausted and starving. Some demanded that the party turn back and would have done so themselves had Walker consented to give them horses and ammunition. He felt that a retreat would lead to disaster and death, whereas going forward might bring them to safe haven. The butchering of horses began. Seventeen were killed before they got out of the mountains.

After several days of struggle "the prospect at this time began to grow somewhat gloomy. We were at a complete stand. No one was acquainted with the country, nor no person knew how wide the summit of this mountain was. We had travelled for five days since we arrived at what we supposed to be the summit, were now still surrounded with snow and rugged peaks, the vigour of every man almost exhausted; nothing to give our poor horses, which were no longer any assistance to us in travelling, but a burthen, for we had to help the most of them along as we would an old and feeble man.

"We travelled a few miles every day, still on top of the mountain, and our course continually obstructed with snow hills and rocks. Here we began to encounter in our path small streams which would shoot out from under these high snow banks and, after running a short distance in deep chasms which they have through ages cut in the rocks, precipitated themselves from one lofty precipice to another, until they are exhausted in rain below. Some of these precipices appeared to us to be more than a mile high." (They were right. Glacier Point is 7,214 feet high, Old Inspiration Point 6,603, Union Point 6,314, and Moran Point 6,258. The famous peaks overlook one of the most beautiful valleys on earth, Yosemite, today a National Park.) "Some of the men thought that if we could succeed in descending one of these precipices to the bottom, we might thus work our way into the valley below, but on making several attempts we found it utterly impossible for a man to descend, to say nothing of our horses." Frustrated in finding a path, "every man appeared to be more discouraged

Toward the end of the Humboldt River

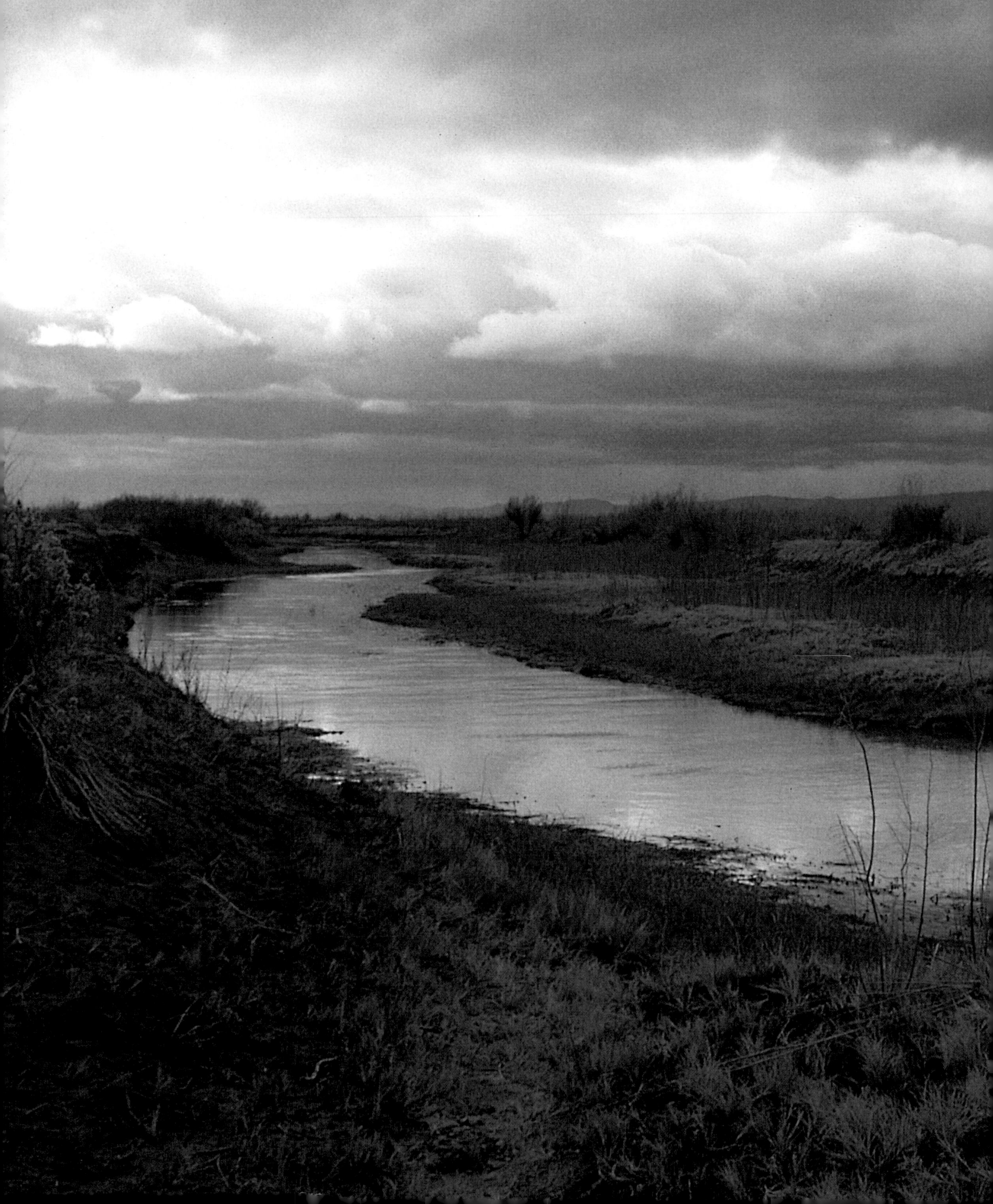

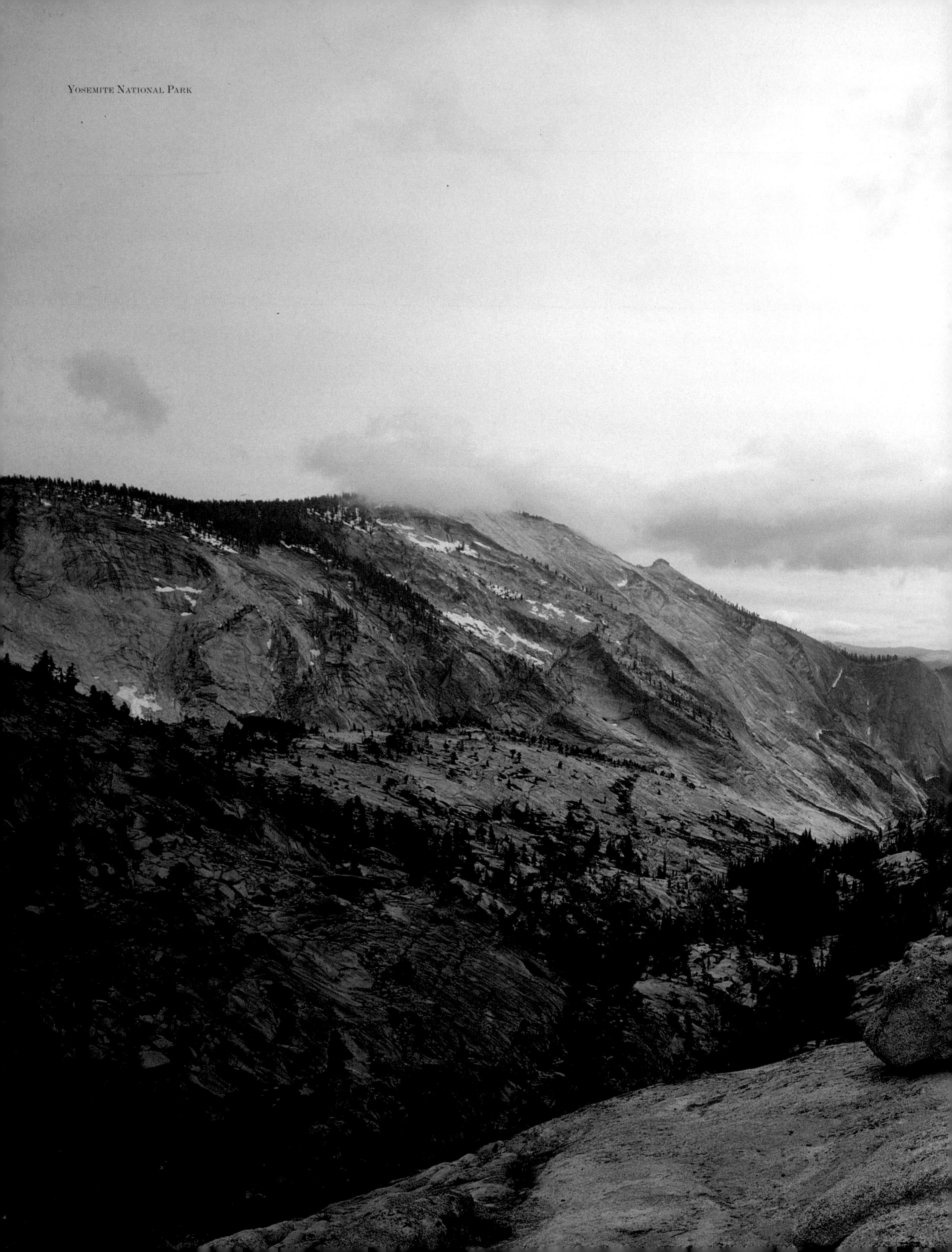

and down-hearted than ever, and I thought that our situation would soon be beyond hope if no prospect of getting from the mountain would now be discovered." Several parties were sent out to reconnoiter daily, and it was a cheerful moment for the men when one came back with a basket full of acorns which had been dropped by an Indian who, on meeting him on the trail, had "run for life. These nuts caused no little rejoicing in our camp, not only on account of their value as food, but because they gave us the gratifying evidence that a country mild and salubrious enough to produce acorns was not far distant."

A few days later they discovered what they thought was an Indian pass that might lead them down and out of the mountains. "We searched for a place that was as smooth and gradual in the descent as possible, and after finding one we brought our horses, and by fastening ropes around them let them down one at a time without doing them any injury. After we got our horses and baggage all over the rocks we continued our course down the mountain, which still continued very steep and difficult. In the evening of the 30th [October] we arrived at the foot or base of this mountain, having spent almost a month in crossing over."

At last they were in the land of legend, and they found it "quite romantic. The soil is very productive, the timber is unusually large and plenty; the game such as deer, elk, grizzly bear and antelopes are remarkably plenty." Traveling in the valley of the Merced River they "found some trees of the red-wood species incredibly large, some of which would measure from 16 to 18 fathoms round the trunk at the height of a man's head from the ground" (Tuolomne Grove).

Joseph Walker "decided that we should forthwith commence trapping for furs and make this expedition as profitable as possible for as yet we had spent much time and toil, and lost many horses, without realizing any profit whatever, although every man expressed himself fully compensated for his labour by the many natural curiosities which we had discovered."

The valley was "swarming with wild horses, some of which are quite docile, particularly the males, on seeing our horses. They are all very fat and can be seen of all colors from spotted to white to jet black; and here, as in the land of civilization, they are the most beautiful and noble, as well as the most valuable of the whole brute creation."

THE REDWOODS IN TUOLOMNE GROVE

YOSEMITE NATIONAL PARK

On their way toward the ocean two nights later the men "were … thrown into great consternation by the singular appearance of the heavens. Soon after dark the air appeared to be completely thickened with meteors falling towards the earth, some of which would explode in the air and others would be dashed to pieces on the ground, frightening our horses so much that it required the most active vigilance of the whole company to keep them together. This was altogether a mystery to some of the men who probably had never before seen or heard of anything of the kind, but after the explanation from Capt. Walker they were satisfied that no danger need be apprehended from the falling of the stars, as they were termed." (It was a remarkable meteoric shower that occurred Nov. 12-13, 1833, and could be observed in much of the United States.)

More wondrous sights awaited them. First, San Francisco Bay, "where it mingles its water with the briny ocean," and then "the broad Pacific burst into view, a smooth unbroken sheet of water which stretched out far beyond the reach of the eye, altogether different from the mountains, rocks, snows and the toilsome plains we had traversed." The following morning "the ocean was not so calm as it was the previous evening. All its sleeping energies were lashed into fury, and the mountain waves of the great deep would roll and dash against the shore, producing the most deafening sound. In the course of the day a detachment of our company was despatched to make discoveries, [and] they found the carcase of a whale which was ninety feet long, the tusks weighing 4½ pounds."

Not long after, "an object … could be dimly seen at a distance riding on the water." It was a ship at sea. "The ship anchored some distance from the shore and the boats were despatched to see what nation we belonged to and what our business was. Their astonishment was equally as great as ours when they ascertained that we were children of the same nation as themselves."

The ship was the *Lagoda* out of Boston, commanded by Captain John Bradshaw. "After exchanging civilities by shaking hands all around, Capt. Baggshaw [as Leonard thought his name to be] strongly insisted on us going on board and partaking of the ship's fare, stating that he had a few casks of untapped Coneac. This was an invitation that none of us had the least desire to refuse."

Walker's men feasted on bread, butter, and cheese, the first they had seen in more than two years, and they drank the cognac with gusto. Walker reciprocated Bradshaw's hospitality the next day. "It was a long time since [the *Lagoda's* crew] had tasted any fresh meat or any thing but salted victuals. After the feasting was at an end, Capt. Baggshaw gave us a description of the country to enable us to lay our plans accordingly."

Walker led his company southward toward Monterey, where he was "forbid trapping in the Indian lands or trading with the natives." After a period of relaxation, Walker and his men decided "to pack up and leave the neighborhood."

The party departed the morning of February 14, 1834, six men electing to stay behind. Walker led his men through the San Joaquin Valley, followed the Kern River (south of today's

Bakersfield), and with the help of two Indian guides, crossed the southern end of the Sierra Nevada Mountains (in the vicinity of Sequoia National Park via what later came to be known as Walker Pass, an important passage for future emigrants to California).

Seeking a shorter way east, he headed into the periphery of the Mojave Desert (on the approach to today's Death Valley National Monument). After two days' hard travel Walker had "no idea how far yet to its termination, and from the manifestations of many of our most valuable stock, we were well convinced they could not endure these hardships much longer." Walker thought they should persist. His men wanted to go back toward the mountains. "Being beloved by the whole company, and being a man also who was seldom mistaken in anything he undertook, the men were very reluctant in going contrary to his will." Walker decided to turn back, thereby avoiding what might have been a fatal trek into the Mojave.

Now in the Owens Valley, heading north, "no signs of our former tracks could be discovered. The compass told which direction we should go, but otherwise we were completely bewildered." Finally, it was their horses that led the men to water, their instinct "far more extensive and more valuable than all the foresight of the men.

"After several days constant travelling we fortunately came to our long sought passage for the west" (east of Yosemite) and then "took a northeast direction keeping our former path, many traces of which were quite visible in places. After continuing our course in this direction without interruption we at length arrived in the neighborhood of the lakes at the mouth of Barren river [the Humboldt Sink], which we had named Battle Lakes."

The company followed the barren Humboldt River, and Walker "decided on leaving this river and taking a northern direction for the purpose of striking the head waters of the Columbia river, where we could find game plenty, and also beaver." After hunting on the Snake River he brought his men back to the Bear River, and on July 12 rejoined Captain Bonneville's company.

Walker remained in the Far West and later served as a guide to the famous explorer and military leader, Captain John Frémont. At his request, the epitaph on his tombstone records that he was the discoverer of Yosemite. It could have recorded many more of his discoveries. Joseph Reddeford Walker left enduring marks on Western exploration, which were memorialized only in part by the naming in his honor of Walker Lake in Nevada, Walker River in Nevada-California, and Walker Pass.

He and his men were the first to blaze a California Trail, first to see the wonderland of Yosemite National Park, first to see Tuolomne Grove's giant redwood trees, and first to reach by land the shores of San Francisco Bay. They were also the first Americans to find, on their return, a gateway through the Sierras, which California-bound emigrants traveled in later years.

------------ Wyeth, 1832-36

The narrative of Wyeth's first expedition to Oregon is based on The Correspondence and Journals of Captain Nathaniel J. Wyeth, 1831-6, *as edited by F. G. Young of the Oregon Historical Society, published in 1899; and* Oregon; or A Short History of a Long Journey from the Atlantic Ocean to the Region of the Pacific, by Land, *published in 1833; the journal was written by Nathaniel's cousin John, who accompanied him only as far as the Rocky Mountains. The early pages of Wyeth's journal, prior to June 6, were found irreparably torn. However, his cousin John's journal provides the details of the first weeks of the trip.*

Chapter 12

NATHANIEL WYETH AND JOHN WYETH: A FOOTHOLD IN OREGON

From the time the Astorians left the Columbia, in 1813, until the appearance there of Jedediah Smith twenty-five years later, the British had seen no American fur-traders in the Pacific Northwest. It might well have remained so if not for Nathaniel Wyeth. Born in Cambridge, in 1802, he grew up during the early era of the trailblazers, reading their exploits and becoming fired with enthusiasm about the West. He was nineteen when the Santa Fe trade began, twenty-six when Jedediah Smith brought his fur-trappers to the Columbia.

When he was thirty years old, Wyeth left his lucrative job in Cambridge and departed to lead a band of New Englanders who, like himself, were totally without experience in wilderness travel, on a historic journey to the West. Their arrival in Oregon marked the turning point in the contest between the United States and Great Britain for eventual sole possession of the Oregon Country.

Wyeth, inspired by a Boston schoolteacher named Hall J. Kelley, the first to be smitten with "Oregon Fever," was a man motivated by grandiose plans for establishing a commercial empire in Oregon which was to have included trapping and trading furs, establishing a salmon fishery, planting tobacco, engaging in large-scale farming, and founding a pioneer settlement. It was a daring, ambitious, and many believed, foolhardy plan considering that he and his party were the quintessential greenhorns.

Wyeth chartered a vessel, the *Sultana,* to sail around the Horn and meet him at the mouth of the Columbia, carrying the supplies and equipment needed for his proposed enterprises.

His small party departed from Boston by ship on March 1, 1832. "The party consisted of 21," wrote John Wyeth, Nathaniel's cousin, "including Nathaniel's brother, Dr. Jacob, and a gunsmith, a blacksmith, two carpenters, and two fishermen, the rest being farmers and laborers brought up to no particular trade. I was the youngest of the company, not having attained my twentieth year." Nathaniel had some unusual ideas about how his party should travel in the wilds. One was that the company should be "uniform in dress. Each one wore a coarse woolen jacket and pantaloons, a striped cotton short, and cowhide boots; every man had a musket, most of them rifles, all of them bayonets in a broad belt, together with a large clasped knife for eating and common purposes." Another of his ideas was that the men should march to the accompaniment of bugle music.

The men sailed to Baltimore, traveled by rail to the Monongahela River, sailed down the river to Pittsburgh, then down the Ohio by steamboat. There was already grumbling and discord. "Passing the rapids of the Ohio, or falls as they are called, between the Indiana Territory and Kentucky, was sufficiently appalling to silence all grumbling. These falls are really terrific to an inexperienced farmer or mechanic. To meet destruction from trees in an immense river seemed to us a danger of life which we had not bargained for, and entirely out of our agreement and calculation. The truth of the matter is . . . the men whom Captain Wyeth had collected were not the sort of men for such an expedition." It was becoming evident, even before the party headed into the wilderness, that this would be a fractious, timorous group of malcontents and dissidents.

At St. Louis they boarded another steamboat and proceeded two hundred and sixty miles up the Missouri river, arriving at Independence, where they were fortunate to join a party under the command of William Sublette. Sublette was leading a supply caravan to the trappers' rendezvous at Pierre's Hole in Idaho. The caravan departed from Independence on May 13 (a few days after Captain Bonneville's wagon train), and on the way to the Platte, the party came to "a large 'prairie,' which name the French have given to extensive tracts of land, mostly level, destitute of trees, and covered with tall, coarse grass."

THE NEBRASKA PRAIRIE WITH SOAPWEED

The Prairie in early June

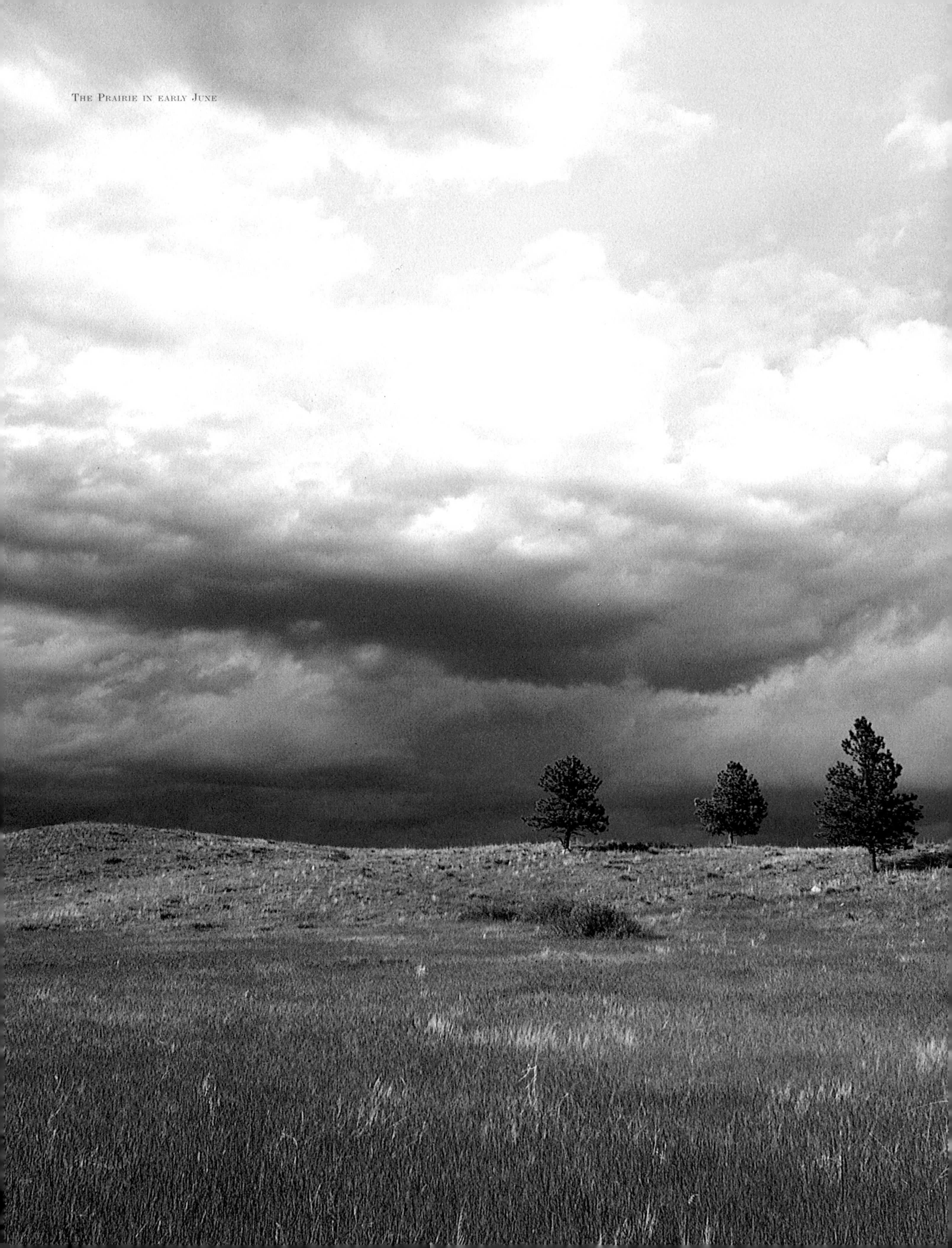

When the caravan arrived at the Platte, cousin John recorded another complaint: "The Missouri Territory is a vast wilderness consisting of immense plains, destitute of wood and water except on the edges of streams that are found near the turbid La Platte. Here were, to be sure, buffaloes, but after we had killed them we had no wood or vegetables of any kind wherewith to kindle a fire for cooking. We were absolutely compelled to dry the dung of the buffalo as the best article we could procure for cooking our coarse beef. That grumbling, discontent and dejection should spring up amongst us no one can be surprised at learning." (Buffalo meat was prized by all other westering travelers and many thought it tasted even better when cooked over "bois de vaches.")

There was yet another problem: " …want of good and wholesome water. The La Platte is warm and muddy, and the use of it occasioned a diarrhea in several of our company. Should the reader wonder how we proceeded so rapidly on our way, he must bear in mind that we were still under the guidance of Captain Sublet[te] who knew every step of the way. To me it seems that we must have perished for want of sustenance in the deserts had we been by ourselves."

At the Black Hills (Laramie Mountains) of Wyoming "our sick suffered extremely in ascending these hills, some of them slipped off the horses and mules they rode on, from sheer weakness brought on by the bowel complaint already mentioned; among these was Dr. Wyeth, our Captain's brother. It was to me particularly grievous to think that he who was to take care of the health of the company was the first who was disabled from helping himself or others."

Nathaniel writes on June 13: "Came in sight of the Black Hills and crossed Laramie Fork of the Platte." Here, Wyeth was responsible for losing a raft containing iron articles and other goods, characterized by John as "a very serious calamity and absolutely irreparable."

When the party reached Pierre's Hole, after crossing the Tetons, Nathaniel wrote: "At the rendezvous of the hunters of this region we found about 120 lodges of the Nez Perces and

SNAKE RIVER OVERLOOK IN THE GRAND TETONS

about 80 of the Flatheads, a company of trappers about 90 under Mr. Dripps of Dripps & Fontenelle connected with the American Fur Co.; many independent hunters and about 100 men of the Rocky Mountain Fur Co. under Mess. Milton Sublette and Mr. Frapp [Henry Fraeb]. I remained at this encampment until the 17th during which time all my men but 11 left me. To these I gave such articles as I could spare from the necessities of my own party and let them go."

Nathaniel Wyeth and the men who chose to stay with him now joined Milton Sublette's twenty-man party, heading westward. But as the parties left the rendezvous a skirmish with some Blackfeet Indians erupted into a bloody conflict that came to be known as the Battle of Pierre's Hole.

On the morning after the battle, Nathaniel and his group "visited the deserted fort; it was a sickening scene of confusion and bloodshead; one of our men, who was killed near their fort, we found mutilated in a shocking manner. We removed back to our former ground to be near our whole force and to recruit the wounded and bury the dead."

John Wyeth had had too much of this sort of life and decided to return home: "Thus ended all my fine prospects and flattering expectations of acquiring fortune, independence, and ease, and all my hopes that the time had now come in the order of Providence, when that uncultivated tract, denominated the Oregon Territory, was to be changed into a fruitful field, and the haunt of savages and wild beasts made the happy abode of refined and dignified men. Mr. Hall J. Kelley published about two years since a most inflated and extravagant account of that western tract which extends from the Rocky Mountains to the shore of the Pacific Ocean. Now the fact is, the sanguine and enthusiastic Mr. Kelley was never in that country, nor nearer to it than Boston; and his zeal in the colonization of that dreary territory led him to believe what he wished, and to disbelieve every thing adverse to his favorite enterprise."

In company with Milton Sublette, the Wyeth party now came to the Snake River at a point before it makes its southward bend, built bull-boats for the crossing, and then, on a route roughly parallel to the Snake, moved across the Gray's River and the Blackfoot River in southeastern Idaho, crossed the Portneuf River near the future site of Pocatello, past the American Falls, and on to the Raft River. Wyeth had ample opportunity to observe Sublette's men trapping beaver, and to learn how to do it. On August 21, he recorded in his journal: "This morning caught my first beaver, a large one."

On August 29, Sublette parted from Wyeth, leading his men on a trapping foray southward, and Nathaniel, for the first time, was on his own in the wilderness; but he was experienced enough to proceed confidently as he headed northward on the long trek toward his Oregon destination. He managed to take his party across the Blue Mountains, and on October 14 he arrived at the Hudson's Bay Company post on the Columbia, Fort Nez Perce, known to Americans as Fort Walla Walla.

"I was received in the most hospitable manner by Peanbron [H. B. Pambrun] the agent for this post" who "gave me a decent change of clothes which was very acceptable. On the 19th

THE BLUE MOUNTAINS, OREGON

I took leave of my hospitable entertainer in one of the Cos. barges with my party, leaving my horses in his charge at the fort, and proceeded down the [Columbia]."At the falls "we hired the Indians about 50 for a quid of tobacco each to carry our boat about 1 mile round the falls, the goods we carried ourselves. After passing the falls we passed what are called the Dalles, small." Wyeth hired more Indians to transport his goods around the Great Dalles. The party made a portage around the Cascades and on the 29th arrived at "the fort of Vancouver."

After their long and arduous trek through the wilderness, the New Englanders had reached their goal. But if there was joy, it was short-lived. Wyeth's men wanted to leave him and, perhaps more importantly, the *Sultana* failed to arrive, stranding him without supplies and equipment to pursue his enterprise. He learned later that the *Sultana* had been shipwrecked at the Society Islands.

Two men decided to stick it out with Wyeth, as "engagés" rather than shareholders, Wiggin Abbott and a man identified only as Woodman. The three went off in a canoe to explore what Wyeth called "the Wallamet or Multnomah River" (the Willamette, a southern tributary of the Columbia). Above the falls of the river Wyeth found "3 or 4 Canadians settled as farmers," and a few more farther along the river; they were former employees of the Hudson's Bay Company, French Canadians, who with their Indian wives, had become the first settlers in the Willamette Valley. Wyeth commented, "I have never seen country of equal beauty except the Kanzas country and I doubt not will one day sustain a large population. If this country is ever colonized this is the point to commence." (It was here that the first Americans established settlements in Oregon, here that Wyeth would stake out a farm on his second expedition.)

OLD GROWTH IN THE WILLAMETTE NATIONAL FOREST

In February, Wyeth and his two hired men joined a Hudson's Bay trapping expedition led by Francis Ermatinger and went up the Columbia to Fort Colville (in northeastern Washington). Here, in an effort to rebuild his shattered business plans, he wrote a letter to George Simpson, the Hudson's Bay governor for all of Canada, proposing a business deal with the giant British fur-trade monopoly. "It appears to me," he wrote, "that as an American I possess some advantage that an Englishman would not inasmuch as I can visit parts of the country from which he is excluded." If Simpson were to supply him with goods, he would trap and trade "south of the Columbia and not within a 100 miles of their posts," and sell furs and skins to the Company at a mutually agreeable price." While waiting for a reply (which came much later, declining his offer), he accompanied Ermatinger southward into Montana, where Wyeth left the British brigade and proceeded to the Snake River.

At the Green River rendezvous Wyeth "found here collected Capt. Walker, Bonneville, Cerry [Cerre] of one Company, Dripps & Fontenelle of the Am[erican] Fur Co., Mr. Campbell [partner of William Sublette in a firm supplying the trappers] just from St. Louis, Mess. Fitzpatric[k], Gervais, Milton Sublette of the Rocky Mountain Fur Co. and in all the Cos. about 300 whites and a small village of Snakes." Wyeth encamped with his old friend, Milton Sublette, who had guided him west from Pierre's Hole.

Wyeth returned to Cambridge, his first expedition to Oregon a commercial failure. He was still convinced, however, that his original intentions of establishing a successful business empire in the West could be achieved. He had, in fact, established a foothold of monumental importance in the eventual occupation of Oregon by the United States. Two of his men who had defected at Fort Vancouver, Solomon Smith and Calvin Tibbetts, had decided to settle in the Willamette Valley. Americans had come to Oregon to stay. And Wyeth would return, bringing settlers. He would bring the first missionaries; others would soon follow. The days of British dominance were numbered.

A detailed report on Wyeth's return to Oregon was made by John Kirk Townsend in his journal,
Narrative of a Journey Across the Rocky Mountains to the Columbia River, *published in*
1839, an account which complements, and amplifies, Nathaniel's somewhat terse journal.

Chapter 13

JOHN TOWNSEND:
WYETH'S RETURN TO OREGON AND THE ARRIVAL OF THE MISSIONARIES

As soon as Nathaniel Wyeth got back to Cambridge, in the fall of 1833, he set to work
organizing his second expedition to Oregon.

He was angered by his cousin John's journal which had just been published, and called it
"one of little lies told for gain." Despite the negativism inspired by John's report, Nathaniel
had no trouble securing the financial backing he needed for his second trip. He arranged for
a brig, the *May Dacre*, "to go round the Horn to bring out some goods and bring home a
cargo of salmon." And he had decided this time to "take across the land about 40 men hired
at the west; men here will not do."

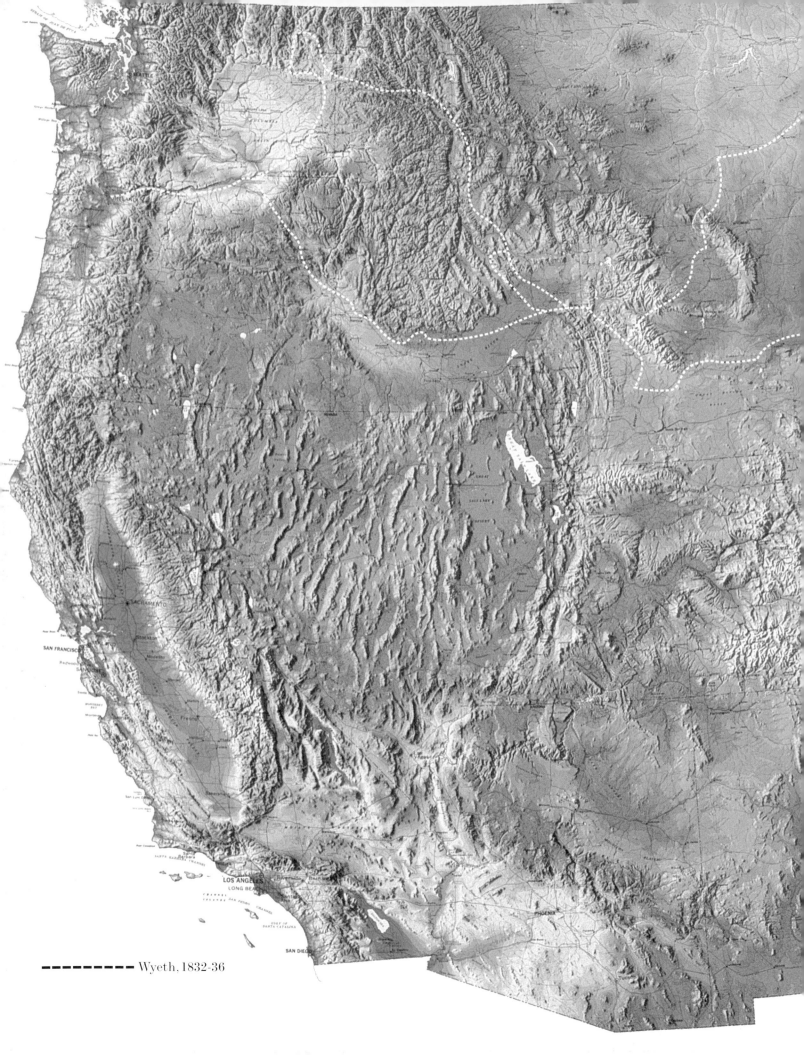

- - - - - - - - - - Wyeth, 1832-36

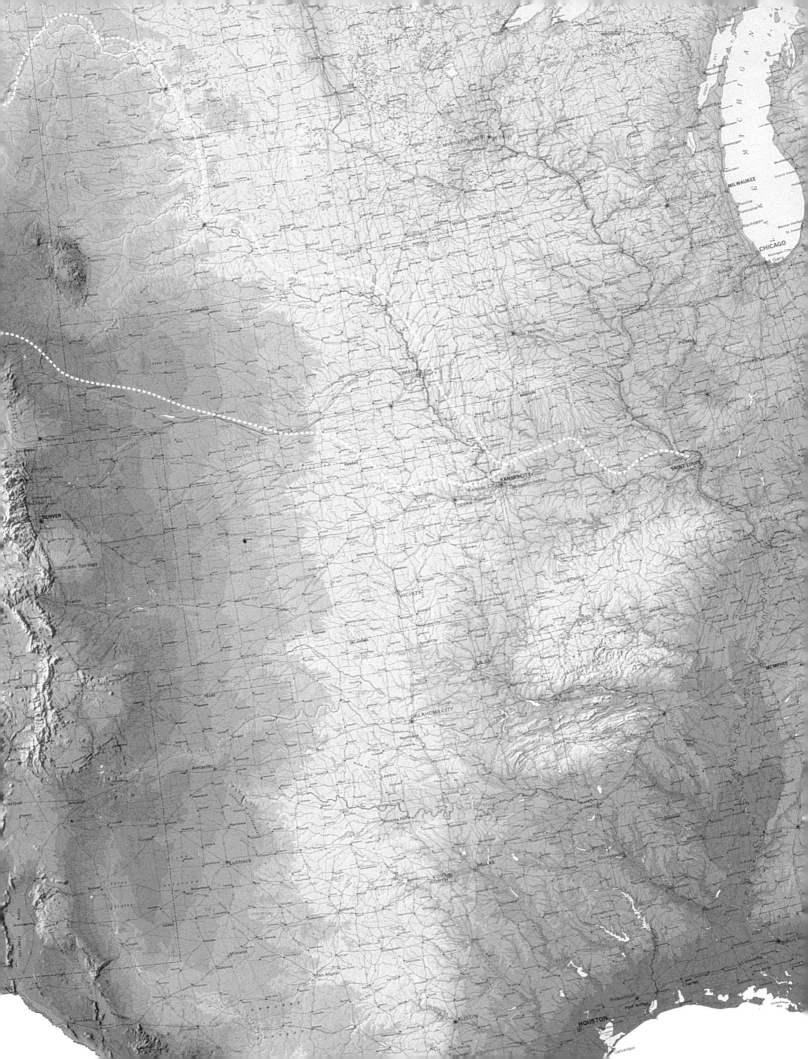

John Kirk Townsend, a twenty-five-year-old Philadelphian, was a physician and ornithologist who joined the expedition at the suggestion of forty-two-year-old Thomas Nuttall, lecturer on botany and zoology at Harvard and veteran of two previous western expeditions. The inclusion of the two natural scientists in the party was one of Nathaniel Wyeth's important contributions to western exploration; the specimens they collected and the reports they made were the first of their kind to emanate from the Far West.

A Methodist missionary, Jason Lee, asked to be allowed to join the expedition, along with his nephew Daniel, also a missionary, and three lay assistants, Cyrus Shepard, Philip Edwards, and Courtney Walker. Their inclusion in the party was to have a profound effect on the future of Oregon. They were to establish missions in the Willamette Valley, around which the first permanent American settlements would spring up.

Milton Sublette and his thirty-man party joined the expedition at Independence, and on April 28, 1834, the large caravan of seventy men and two hundred fifty horses began the march. But Sublette had developed a mysterious leg ailment, and on May 8, turned back. "His departure has thrown a gloom over the whole camp," noted Townsend.

The route of the expedition would be along the North Platte to the Sweetwater, and across the Rockies at South Pass—a long stretch of what would soon come to be known as the Oregon Trail.

Wyeth led the caravan across the plains, making good time and encountering no serious problems. On the thirteenth day, just before the party reached the Blue River, a curious incident occurred and was noted by Townsend: "Our scouts came in this morning with the intelligence that they had found a large trail of white men, bearing N.W. We have no doubt that this is Wm. Sublette's party [brother of Milton] and that it passed us last evening. They must have been travelling very rapidly to overtake us so soon, and no doubt had men ahead watching our motions. It seems rather unfriendly, perhaps, to run by us in this furtive way, without even stopping to say good morning, but Sublette is attached to a rival company, and all stratagems are deemed allowable when interest is concerned. It is a matter of some moment to be the first at the mountain rendezvous, in order to obtain the furs brought every summer by the trappers."

But there was more to it than that, as Nathaniel Wyeth uneasily perceived. He suspected that William Sublette had some ulterior motive for trying to reach Thomas Fitzpatrick at the rendezvous. He dispatched a message to Fitzpatrick, with whom he had a trade agreement: "Wm. Sublette having passed me here, I am induced to write to you and hope you will get it. You may expect me by the 1st July at the rendezvous. I am not heavily loaded and shall travel as fast as possible and have a sufficient equipment of goods for you according to contract."

On June 1, at the crossing of the Laramie River, Wyeth noted, "we found 13 of Sublette's men camped for the purpose of building a fort, he having gone ahead with his best animals and the residue of his goods." (First named Fort William, then Fort John, the post subsequently became Fort Laramie, a major caravansary on the Oregon Trail, and a base of military operations against the Indians.)

The Oregon Trail in Wyoming

145

Some days later, Wyeth wrote another note to Fitzpatrick, confirming that he was approaching, and indirectly reminding him again of their contract.

The caravan passed the Red Buttes (near Casper, Wyoming) where, as Wyeth noted in his journal, "we leave to strike for [the] Sweet Water." Both Wyeth and Townsend noted their encampment at Independence Rock. "Like the Red Buttes," wrote Townsend, "this rock is also a rather remarkable point in the route. On its smooth perpendicular sides we see carved the names of most of the mountain 'bourgeois' [the term then used for the boss of an expedition or a trading post]." They saw that among the names was that of William Sublette and the date of his encampment. Wyeth and Townsend both inscribed their names on Independence Rock.

The crossing of the Rockies via South Pass went unremarked by either diarist, both apparently taking this safe passage through the mountains very much for granted. Wyeth simply mentioned "16 miles over broken ground," and Townsend observed that it was "a hard and toilsome march for both man and beast." They made camp on Sandy River and proceeded to Green River, arriving at the rendezvous on June 19.

Townsend had come down with "a violent fever, sickness, and pain," and his description of the rendezvous reflects his mood. He describes "these people, with their obstreperous mirth, their whooping and howling and quarreling, added to the mounted Indians, who are constantly dashing into and through our camp yelling like fiends, the barking and baying of savage wolf-dogs, and the incessant cracking of rifles and carbines, render our camp a perfect bedlam."

To Wyeth's dismay, Fitzpatrick repudiated the contract they had previously made. "These circumstances have induced me to quit their neighborhood as soon as possible." A letter to his uncle revealed how he would try to recover his fortunes: " . . . I am obliged to establish a fort which I shall do on Lewis [Snake] River about a hundred miles west of this for the purpose of trading my goods [with the Indians], and then leave part of my men at it and then proceed to the Columbia for the further prosecution of the business."

When the rendezvous broke up, the missionary Jason Lee decided to accompany Wyeth to the Columbia, abandoning his original plan of establishing a mission among the Flathead Indians in Montana—a decision that would change the course of American history by initiating the continuing settlement of Oregon. The caravan headed for the confluence of the Portneuf and Snake rivers, where Wyeth proposed to build his trading post—another event that would change the course of American history. Now the expedition was back on the Oregon Trail, and Wyeth's trading post, Fort Hall, would become one of its most important stops.

On July 8 the party reached Soda Springs on the Bear River. Townsend noted that the taste of the "strong supercarbonated water" in the several springs "which bubble up with all the activity of artificial fountains" was "very agreeable and refreshing, resembling Saratoga water, but not so saline." Trappers who came upon the springs enjoyed the taste of the waters so much that they called the site Beer Springs. Wyeth, on the other hand, noted that it tasted like "bilge water."

INSCRIBED NAMES ON THE OREGON TRAIL

On July 15, Wyeth reached the Portneuf and began building his trading post, while, at the mouth of the Boise River, the missionaries went on ahead.

Several weeks later the expedition left the new post, crossed the Snake River Plain— a difficult, arid, desert stretch, and came to what was then known as Godin's Creek (now Lost River, to the east of today's lava-filled Craters of the Moon National Monument).

While crossing the mountains (of Boise National Forest) Wyeth had a near-fatal accident. "I climbed up the clefts," he wrote, "and in passing over the snow had liked to have been killed, in the following manner. Passing over some snow and on which the water was running, and being afraid of caving in, I missed my foothold in a slippery place and went gradually sliding down to a precipice, but succeeded at last in averting my progress to destruction by catching the only stone which projected above the snow."

Of the descent Wyeth tersely noted, "A very steep trail—about the worst road that I ever passed." Townsend had more to say about it: "The whole journey today has been a most fearful one. For myself I might have diminished the danger very considerably by adopting

EAST BUTTE ON THE SNAKE RIVER PLAIN

SAWTOOTH NATIONAL FOREST

the plan pursued by the rest of the company, that of walking and leading my horse over the most dangerous places, but I have been suffering for several days with a lame foot and am wholly incapable of such exertion. So I dropped the rein upon the animal's neck and allowed him to take his own course, closing my eyes and keeping as quiet as possible in the saddle. But I could not forbear starting occasionally, when the feet of my horse would slip on a stone, and one side of him would slide rapidly towards the edge of the precipice, but I always recovered myself by a desperate effort, and it was fortunate for me that I did so."

Emerging from the mountains, the party struck the Boise River, which Townsend noted was "literally crowded with salmon, which are springing from the water almost constantly. Our mouths are watering most abundantly for some of them, but we are not provided with

SPAWNING PINK SALMON

ELKHORN RIDGE, BLUE MOUNTAINS

suitable implements for taking any, and must therefore depend for a supply on the Indians, whom we hope soon to meet." They soon did, coming upon a village of Shoshones.

Wyeth had some difficulty crossing the mountains of eastern Oregon north of the Powder River, on what he termed the "Walla Walla Trail." The party was lost for two days while Wyeth searched for, and finally found, the trail near one he had "descended on my first tour."

In the Grande Ronde valley, Townsend noted, "we found Captain Bonneville's company, which had been lying here several days, waiting the arrival of its trapping parties." From the Grande Ronde, Wyeth led his party across the Blue Mountains and down the Umatilla River to the Walla Walla, reaching Fort Walla Walla at the confluence of the Columbia on September 2. Wyeth's troubles, however, had not come to an end. The brig *May Dacre* arrived too late for the salmon season, on which Wyeth was depending. Still persevering, he now set about building a post, which he called Fort William, on Sauvie's Island (known then as Wappatoo Island) near the mouth of the Columbia. He laid out a farm on the banks of the river some forty miles above and despatched trappers. With another party he set off to trap along the Des Chutes River. Townsend had arrived at Fort Vancouver in mid-September, finding the missionaries there. Shortly after, they chose for their mission site French Valley, where several French-Canadians, former voyageurs of the Hudson's Bay Company, had settled. It became the nucleus of American pioneer settlement. Nathaniel Wyeth, meanwhile, found only frustration and failure. He remained in Oregon until the end of September, trying to reestablish himself, but he knew his venture had failed.

Fort William was abandoned and used as a farm by the Hudson's Bay Company, which bought Fort Hall from Wyeth. The British maintained Fort Hall, selling supplies and provisions, at high prices, to travelers on the Oregon Trail, until the United States took sole possession of the Oregon Territory in 1846, after which it became a military post.

On his return to the East, Wyeth met one Samuel Parker on the Columbia, and provided him with a vocabulary of the Chinook language. Farther east he passed a caravan bringing the missionaries Marcus Whitman and Henry Spalding to Oregon. With them were their wives, Narcissa and Elizah, the first white women to travel the Oregon Trail, another significant harbinger of settlement.

When Wyeth returned to Boston, he was welcomed back to his old business. The curtain had closed on the drama of Nathaniel Wyeth's adventures in Oregon, but it was rising, thanks to his efforts, on the drama of those whom he had brought to Oregon and those who, led by the missionaries, soon followed in their footsteps.

In his last mention of Nathaniel Wyeth, John Townsend wrote: "Captain Wyeth has pursued the plans which seemed to him best adapted for insuring success with the most indefatigable perseverance and industry, and has endured hardships without murmuring, which would have prostrated many a more robust man; nevertheless he has not succeeded in making the business of fishing and trapping productive, and as we cannot divine the cause we must attribute it to the Providence that rules the destinies of men and controls all human enterprise."

In his Journal of an Exploring Tour Beyond the Rocky Mountains, *published in 1838, Rev. Samuel Parker narrated the extraordinary journey undertaken by him to scout appropriate sites for the establishment of missions. It is one of the most articulate and discerning of the early chronicles of the West.*

One of the best descriptions of Fort Vancouver, an impressive establishment, a huge trading post, a self-sufficient mini-city, appeared in a journal written by Thomas Farnham, Travels in the Great Western Prairie, *which covered his 1839 journey to Oregon.*

Chapter 14

SAMUEL PARKER: THE MISSIONARY TRAILBLAZER

Samuel Parker was fifty-six, a father of three teen-agers, a veteran of many years' missionary service on the western frontiers of New York, and a dominie at an Ithaca school for girls, when he suddenly decided to go to Oregon to establish missions for the Christian salvation of the Indians.

Along with thirty-two-year-old Marcus Whitman, a country doctor with a calling to serve as a Presbyterian medical missionary in the Far West, Parker joined a caravan to the Rockies from Liberty, Missouri, early in May 1835, led by Lucien Fontenelle.

The travelers reached Fort Bellevue, a trading post near Council Bluffs, then traveled along the Platte. Whitman writes of eastern Nebraska, in the vicinity of Omaha: "It is rich bottom land, covered with a luxuriant growth of grass. No country could be more inviting to the farmer, with only one exception, the want of woodland. The time will come, and probably is not far distant, when this country will be covered with a dense population."

On the North Platte the caravan passed the arresting landmarks of the Oregon Trail and Parker's descriptions of them were among the first to be published.

Of what was known as Court House Rock: "The old castle, which is a great natural curiosity, had all the appearance of an old enormous building, somewhat dilapidated; but still you see the standing walls, the roof, the turret, embrasures, the dome, and almost the very windows."

Of Chimney Rock: "Another of nature's wonders. It has been called the Chimney, but I should say it ought to be called Beacon Hill from its resemblance to Beacon Hill in Boston. It has a conical formed base of about half a mile in circumference, and one hundred and fifty feet in height; and above this a perpendicular column twelve feet square and eight feet high."

Of Scott's Bluffs: "These are the termination of a high range of land running from south to north. They are very near the river, high and abrupt, and what is worthy of notice, there is a pass through the range a short distance back from the river, the width of a common road, with perpendicular sides two or three hundred feet high."

(John Townsend, who had passed these landmarks with Nathaniel Wyeth, had described a bluff bearing "a striking and almost startling resemblance to a dilapidated feudal castle" — Court House Rock — and "a kind of obelisk tapering to a small point at the top" — Chimney Rock. He had also mentioned "a large and deep ravine between the enormous bluffs.

JAIL AND COURT HOUSE ROCKS

CHIMNEY ROCK

It was a most enchanting sight; even the men noticed it, and more than one of our matter-of-fact people exclaimed, 'beautiful beautiful!' (These are called Scott's Bluffs, so named from an unfortunate trader, who perished here from disease and hunger, many years ago. He was deserted by his companions, and the year following, his crumbling bones were found in this spot.)"

The caravan's arrival at Fort William (which Wyeth and Townsend had seen being built by William Sublette, and which came to be known as Fort Laramie) was where Parker said good-bye to Fontenelle, who remained at the fort. The missionaries were placed in the capable hands of Tom Fitzpatrick for the next leg of their trek, across the Rockies to the Green River rendezvous, where they met Jim Bridger. (The veteran mountain-man had a three-inch long arrowhead embedded in his back, a painful souvenir of a skirmish with Blackfeet Indians three years before; Marcus Whitman removed the arrowhead.)

At the rendezvous, Utaws, Shoshones, Nez Perces, and Flatheads sat in council with Parker and Whitman, who "enquired whether they wished to have teachers come among them and instruct them in the knowledge of God, his worship, and the way to be saved." A Nez Perce chief said that he "had heard from white men a little about God, which had only gone into his ears; he wished to know enough to have it go down into his heart, to influence his life, and to teach his people."

Whitman went back to the East with the promise he would bring associates the following year to establish a mission. Parker would continue with a convoy of Indians to guide him to Fort Walla Walla on the Columbia River.

It was now Jim Bridger's turn to shepherd Parker and his flock of Nez Perce Indians to Jackson Hole and across the Tetons. The journey became increasingly difficult for the aging missionary. Crossing into Idaho over Teton Pass, Parker found himself "on a zigzag trail often inclined at an angle of 45 degrees toward the stream below."

Some weeks later, as the party approached the site of Lewiston, Idaho, one of the Nez Perce Indians asked Parker if he thought the spot was "good for missionaries to live in." Parker thought it was. (Marcus Whitman and Henry Spalding came into the area the following year, and Spalding and his wife established a mission in the Lapwai Valley of the Clearwater River.)

When Parker reached Fort Walla Walla he was warmly welcomed by the ever-hospitable Pierre Pambrun, but after only two days' rest he left the Nez Perces by canoe for Fort Vancouver, two hundred miles down the Columbia. "The Falls and La Dalles furnish a situation for water power equal to any in any part of the world." (The falls and rapids, around which he and so many other early travelers to the mouth of Columbia were forced to detour by portage, lie today under deep waters caused by dams erected to control the water power for electric generating plants.)

THE COLUMBIA RIVER

"At the lower part of the La Dalles I found Capt. Wyeth from Boston, who is an intelligent and sociable man." Wyeth told him about his many failures and disasters, and probably about the activities of Jason Lee and his missionary companions on the Willamette, whom Parker would soon meet.

On October 16, Parker arrived at the impressive Fort Vancouver, a huge trading post, a self-sufficient mini-city, described as follows by Thomas Farnham, a member of the first non-missionary group to travel to Oregon for the purpose of settlement: "The fort itself is an oblong square 250 yards in length by 150 in breadth, enclosed by pickets 20 feet in height. The area within is divided into two courts, around which are arranged 35 wooden buildings used as officers' dwellings, lodging apartments for clerks, storehouses for furs, goods and grains; and as workshops for carpenters, blacksmiths, coopers, tinners, wheelwrights, etc. One building near the rear gate is occupied as a school house; and a brick structure as a powder magazine. Six hundred yards below the fort, and on the bank of the river, is a village of 52 wooden houses [in which] live the company's servants. Among them is a hospital.

"And behold the Vancouver farm, stretching up and down the river . . . 3,000 acres, fenced in beautiful fields, sprinkled with dairy houses, and herdsmen and shepherds' cottages! A busy place is this." There were Iroquois Indians working in the fields, Sandwich Islanders felling timber for the saw-mill, a grist mill furnishing "bread stuff for the posts and the Russian market in the northwest." Farnham was impressed also, as Samuel Parker must have been, by the baronial manner in which Dr. John McLoughlin, executive officer of the Hudson's Bay Company in the territory west of the Rocky mountains, ruled over his fiefdom.

After adjusting himself to his luxurious environment in such unexpected contrast to his trek through the wilderness, Parker decided to do some sight-seeing on "the lower part of the river and the sea coast, and return before the rainy season should commence; and also to avail myself of a passage in the *May Dacre* of Boston . . . a brig belonging to Capt. Wyeth and Company, which was lying twenty-five miles below, at the lowest mouth of the Multnomah [the Willamette]. Mr. J. K. Townsend, an ornithologist from Philadelphia accompanied me to the brig."

While waiting for the brig to set sail, Parker "made a long excursion through woods and prairies" in the valley of the Willamette. He was impressed with its potential, and wondered: "When will this immensely extended and fertile country be brought under cultivation, and be filled with an industrious population?" (He was at the site of Oregon City, and only about twelve miles from that of Portland.)

The *May Dacre* brought Parker to the historic site at the mouth of the Columbia, Fort Astoria. Parker went ashore to visit, finding that the fort "is without fortifications, has only two small buildings made of hewed logs, about two acres cleared, a part of which is cultivated with potatoes and green vegetables. It is occupied by two white men of the Hudson Bay Company, for the purpose of trade with the few remaining Indians who reside about these shores."

For the next few months Parker made his residence at Fort Vancouver. He made another excursion to the Willamette Valley and visited the Lees at their missionary station. "There is as yet one important desideratum—these missionaries have no wives. Christian white women are very much needed to exert their influence over Indian females."

In the spring, Parker departed from Fort Vancouver and went to Fort Walla Walla and as far as the Snake River, but declined to be taken back into the Salmon River Mountains where he had been so sick on his trip west. He returned to Walla Walla.

There Parker was offered a tour of the Hudson's Bay Company posts in the Spokane country. He traveled to the Spokane River, visited Fort Colville, which he thought would be a good site for a mission, enjoyed a "fine view of Kettle Falls—a sublime spectacle," visited Fort Okanagan, "first built by Mr. David Stuart [the Astorian] in 1811," and was back at Fort Vancouver by mid-June.

Soon after, he was given free passage on a Hudson's Bay Company vessel to the Sandwich Islands, and after a stay of five months, he sailed for home.

"Oregon Fever" was now spreading in communities east of the Mississippi. Jason Lee had brought settlers there, and would recruit more. Marcus Whitman, traveling with his wife and accompanied by the Spaldings and by William Gray, chose their sites in the countryside of the Columbia. In May 1837, another nucleus of settlement arrived by ship at the Columbia, a party of reinforcements from the east to join Jason Lee in the Willamette Valley. William Gray returned to western New York and persuaded another group of missionaries to come to the West in the spring of 1838. John Sutter, a Swiss emigrant looking for opportunities in the West, was on that trip. After a reconnoiter of Oregon, he headed for California where he established Sutter's Fort on the Sacramento River. The first non-missionary group, fifteen men led by Thomas Farnham, went overland from Peoria, Illinois.

From now on the settlers would keep coming. The United States would soon move to protect travel on the Oregon Trail and assure American possession of Oregon.

MT. HOOD

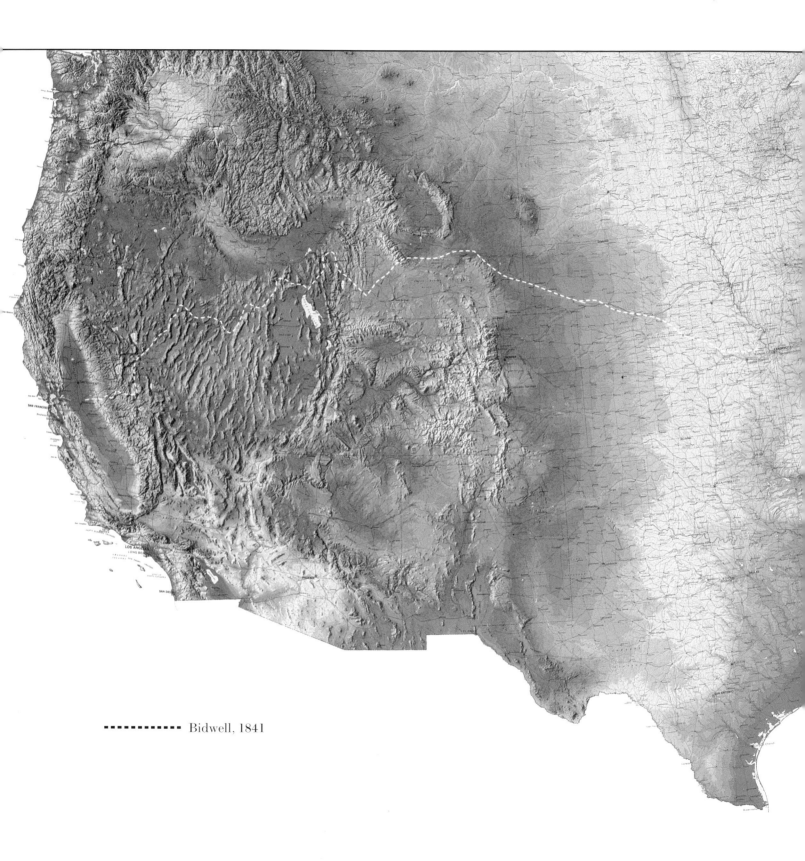

Bidwell, 1841

John Bidwell described what happened in his Echoes of the Past about California, *written many years after his experiences.*
Nicholas Dawson, late in life, wrote about his experiences in the Narrative of Nicholas "Cheyenne" Dawson. *His book complements Bidwell's as a source for the historic trek.*

Chapter 15

BIDWELL AND DAWSON: FIRST EMIGRANT PARTY TO CALIFORNIA

Settlement of California by emigrants began in 1841, although before that several hardy souls had found their way there. Glowing reports filtered back, fueling the flames of interest and, coupled with the financial depression from which the nation had only begun to emerge in 1840, motivating many to consider a new start in the West.

The era of the emigrant had already opened in Oregon, where Americans had a legal right to settle. But California was foreign soil, in the possession of Mexico, which had declared independence from Spain in 1821. The emigrants, since they had been allowed by the Mexicans to colonize Texas (and had, in 1836, declared Texas an independent republic), thought they would have no problem settling California.

John Bidwell, who taught school near Fort Leavenworth, Kansas, was one who joined the newly formed Western Emigration Society and, by May of 1841, found himself on his way west. Twenty-two-year-old Nicholas Dawson, an Ohioan who had come to Missouri three years before with "an overweaning desire to travel," was also among the party, a mixed crowd having little in common aside from their inexperience. So inexperienced were they that, not knowing how to begin, they waited for "a company of Catholic missionaries ... with an old Rocky Mountaineer for a guide" (Thomas Fitzpatrick) to show them the way.

CHIMNEY ROCK, NEBRASKA

"In general," Bidwell wrote, "our route lay from near Westport, where Kansas City now is, northwesterly over the prairie, crossing several streams, till we struck the Platte River. Then we followed along the south side of the Platte and a day's journey or so along the South Fork. Then crossing the South Fork and following up the north side for a day or so we went over to the North Fork and camped at Ash Hollow; thence up the north side of that fork, passing those noted landmarks known as the Court House Rocks, Chimney Rock, Scott's Bluffs etc., till we came to Fort Laramie, a trading post of the American Fur Company;

thence after several days we came to another noted landmark called Independence Rock, on a branch of the North Platte called the Sweetwater, which we followed up to the head [over the South Pass], soon after striking the Big Sandy, which empties into Green River. Next we crossed Green River to Black Fork, which we followed up till we came to Ham's Fork, at the head of which we crossed the divide between Green and Bear rivers. Then we followed Bear River down to Soda Spring." (To this point the party had followed the Oregon Trail. Beyond this point it would turn to find a way to California.)

THE OREGON TRAIL IN WYOMING

The party, led by Captain John Bartleson, reached the Green River on July 23. Dawson noted: "Our journey from here to Soda Springs, on Bear River, was more difficult—more mountains and fewer valleys. At times we could pass along the mountain sides only by having fastened to the top of our loads ropes to which men clung to keep the load from tipping the wagon over, and we descended steeps by having behind the wagons men clinging to ropes. At Soda Springs we parted company with the crowd that was going to Oregon, which crowd included Fitzpatrick and the priests. Thirty-one of us, including one woman, Mrs. Benjamin Kelsey, and her child, decided to strike out for California.

"We knew nothing positive of the route, except that it went west. There was but one man in the mountains that had ever been to California—and he was supposed to be at Fort Hall on Snake River. So we sent two men to the fort for [the man] Walker, and the rest of us were to travel leisurely down Bear River until we reached a beautiful valley which the trappers called Cache, and there await their return.

"The two men came without Walker but brought word that we must be careful in searching for Ogden [Humboldt] River to avoid falling over into feeders of Snake river, lest we should get into the canyons without grass or water."

Bidwell: "[Our men] brought the information that we must strike out west of Salt Lake, being careful not to go too far south lest we should get into a wasteless country without grass. They also said we must be careful not to go too far north, lest we should get into a broken country and steep canyons, and wander about, as trapping parties had been known to do, and become bewildered and perish."

Difficult and dangerous stretches of the trek now lay ahead. No maps to help; no guides to lead. Only the advice from Fort Hall that they must find the Humboldt River and follow it westward.

Bidwell wrote: "The principal growth, on plain and hill alike, was the interminable sagebrush, and often it was difficult, for miles at a time, to break a road through it, and sometimes a lightly laden wagon would be overturned. We traveled all day without water, and at midnight found ourselves in a plain as level as a floor, incrusted with salt and as white as snow. Crusts of salt broken up by our wagons and driven by the chilly night wind like ice on the surface of the water of a frozen pond was to me a striking counterfeit of a winter scene. This plain became softer and softer until our poor, almost famished animals could not pull our wagons. The condition of our animals compelled us to rest nearly a week."

Two men were sent out to hunt for the Humboldt while the others waited near Pilot Peak on the Utah-Nevada border. The river was found but wagons could not travel the route. "We turned southward around the northwest corner of the [Great Salt] lake, and found a pass where, by roping them, we took the wagons through ... Our valley was charming but the line of mountains ahead of us [the Ruby Mountains of Nevada] seemed unbroken by a pass. We held a consultation that night and decided to abandon our wagons here, and make pack saddles, and pack through."

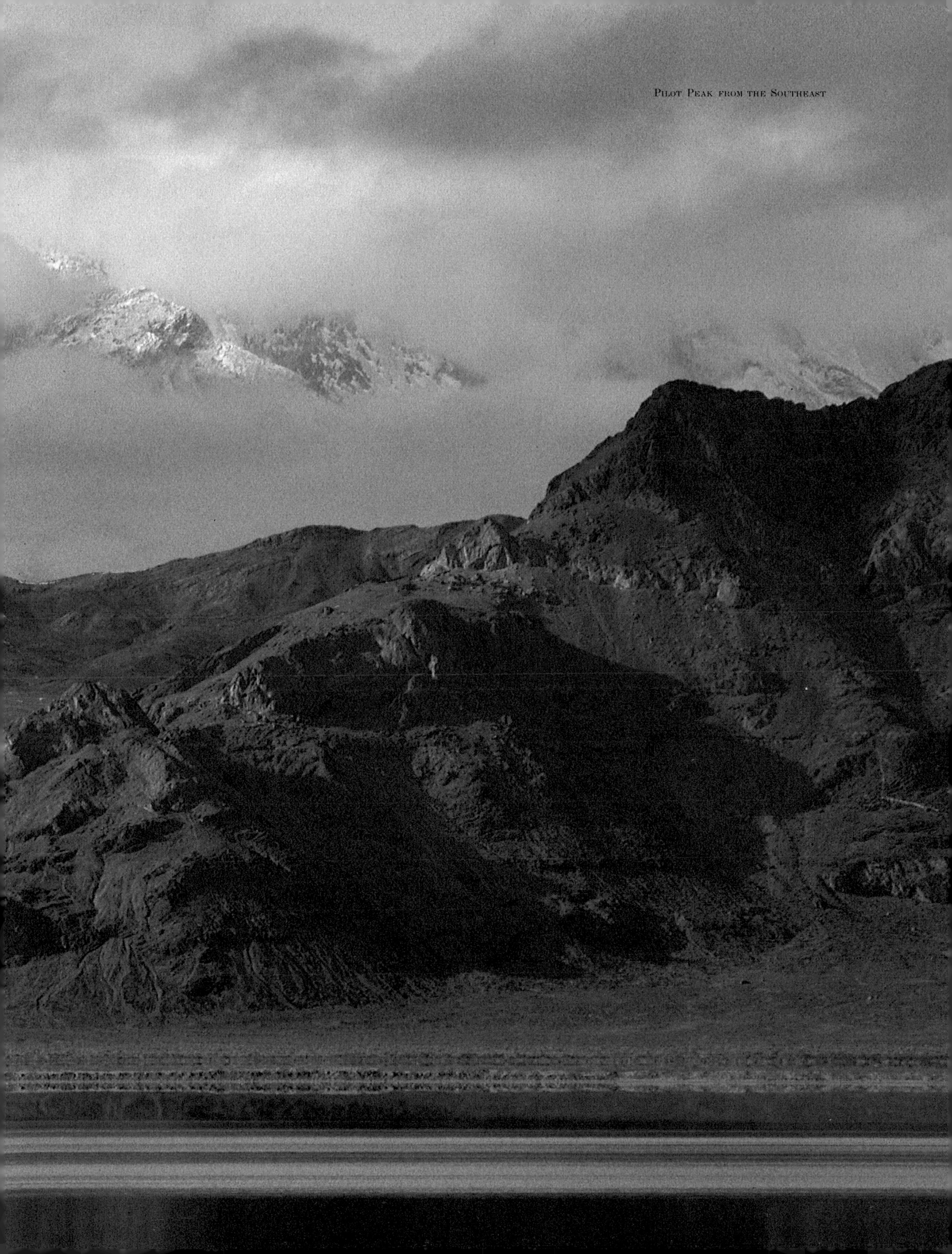

Pilot Peak from the Southeast

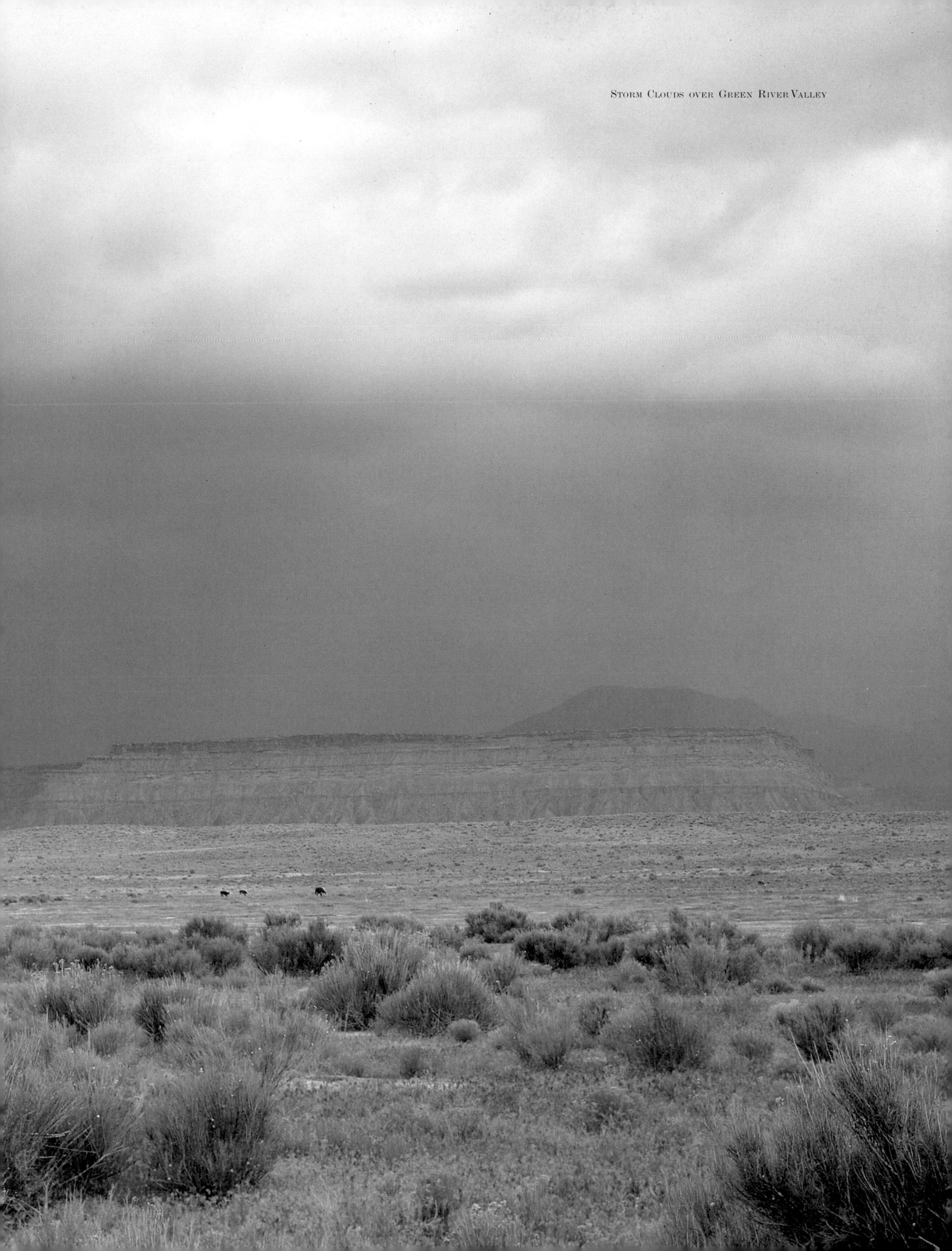

Storm Clouds over Green River Valley

In the Great Basin of Nevada the trek to the Humboldt River was arduous and exhausting. "We entered a canyon, the walls of which were precipitous and several hundred feet high. Finally the pleasant bermy banks gave out entirely, and we could travel only in the dry bed of what in the wet season was a raging river. It became a solid mass of stones and huge boulders, and the animals became tenderfooted and sore so that they could hardly stand up, and as we continued the way became worse and worse."

Dawson wrote: "Wearily, and with much trouble with our packs, we made our way to the Ogden … since the Humboldt … and down it … the country on both sides appeared a desert. The river seemed to be dwindling instead of receiving big tributaries to swell its flood and guide us into the plains of California and on to the Pacific … But the route was becoming more nearly impassable; and, alas! what meant those big mountains ahead with no opening through them?"

When the party arrived at the mountains of the Humboldt Range, dissension between Bidwell and Captain Bartleson caused a rupture. The party split into two and, as Bidwell says, his group was "thrown entirely upon our own resources. By following our fugitive captain and party across the Humboldt, we thereby missed the luxuriant Truckee meadows lying but a short distance to the west, a resting place well and favorably known to later emigrants. So, perforce, we followed down to the Sink of the Humboldt [east of today's Reno, Nevada] and were obliged to drink its water, which in the fall of the year becomes stagnant and the color of lye, and not fit to drink or use unless boiled."

By the time they reached "the very eastern base of the Sierra Nevada," Bidwell wrote: " … we had only two oxen left. We sent men ahead to see if it would be possible to scale the mountains, while we killed the better of the two oxen and dried the meat in preparation for the ascent." The men returned toward evening and reported that they thought it would be possible, though very difficult. After supper that evening they got "ready to climb in the morning." Bartleson and his group, which included Dawson, unexpectedly came up, and the entire party headed for the mountains, although traveling separately.

Bidwell: "We were now in what is at present Nevada, and probably within forty miles of the present boundary of California. We ascended the mountain on the north side of Walker River to the summit and then struck a stream running west which proved to be the extreme source of the Stanislaus River. We followed it down for several days and finally came to where a branch ran into it, each forming a canyon."

Dawson: "One day while we were going down a ridge between two conveying streams we saw ahead high cliffs with a narrow opening between them. We suspicioned a canyon and halted, for we knew that if we were unable when we reached that point to go on, that neither men nor animals would have the strength to climb back up the slope. We sent two men, Bidwell and Jimmy Johns, ahead to explore. Bidwell returned alone and reported that only a bird could go through."

Bidwell:"When Jimmy and I got down about three-quarters of a mile I came to the conclusion that it was impossible to get through and said to him,'Jimmy, we might as well go back; we can't go here.' 'Yes, we can,' said he, and insisting that we could, he pulled out a pistol and fired."[This was intended as a signal that the rest of the party should follow them into the canyon.] "I hurried back to tell the company not to come down, but before I reached them the captain and his party had started. I explained, and warned them that they could not get down but they went on as far as they could go and then were obliged to stay all day and all night to rest the animals, and had to go among the rocks and pick a little grass for them, and go down to a stream through a terrible place in the canyon to bring water up in cups and camp kettles, and some of the men in their boots, to pour down the animals' throats in order to keep them from perishing. Finally, four of them pulling and four pushing a mule, they managed to get them up one by one, and then carried all the things up again on their backs—not an easy job for exhausted men.

"In some way, nobody knows how, Jimmy got through that canyon and into the Sacramento Valley. He had a horse with him, an Indian horse that was bought in the Rocky Mountains, and which could come as near climbing a tree as any horse I ever knew. Jimmy was a character. Of all the men I have ever known I think he was the most fearless; he had the bravery of a bulldog."

Dawson:"One day a stark naked Indian came into camp, and as he was very friendly, we employed him to pilot us. He led us along shelves of rocks which overhung vast precipices. Here and there great rocks projected over the path and frequently a pack would strike one of these rocks and over the precipice would go pack and animal, and be lost to us entirely. We all went on foot, leading our animals. Once when I was struggling along to keep Monte [his Indian pony] from going over, I looked back and saw Mrs. Kelsey a little way behind me, with her child [one-year-old Ann] in her arms, barefooted, I think, and leading her horse— a sight I shall never forget. Well, our pilot deserted us when we reached the stream. I suppose to go back and plunder the animals that had fallen off the bluffs."

Bidwell:"We went on, traveling as near west as we could. When we killed our last ox we shot and ate crows or anything we could kill, and one man shot a wildcat. We could eat anything. We were now on the edge of the San Joaquin Valley, but we did not even know that we were in California. We could see a range of mountains lying to the west, the Coast Range, but we could see no valley."

Dawson:"Instead of plains and a big ocean, there ahead were big mountains, and we had come to hate mountains."

Bidwell:"The evening of the day we started down into the valley we were very tired, and when night came our party was strung along for three or four miles, and every man slept where darkness overtook him. When we overtook the foremost of the party the next morning we found they had come to a pond of water and one of them had killed a fat coyote. When I came up it was all eaten except the lights and the windpipe, on which I made my

COYOTE

breakfast." But now the ordeal was at an end, for that day they descended into the valley.

MOUNT DIABLO

In the valley, Bidwell noted, the party found abundant game, "killed fifteen deer and antelopes, jerked the meat, and got ready to go on. It was now about the first of November. Our party set forth bearing northwest, aiming for a seeming gap north of a high mountain in the chain to the west of us. That mountain we found to be Mount Diablo."

Dawson: "We were traveling alone, pretty comfortable on the whole, but casting glances of anxiety toward the mountains ahead, when we saw two men approaching ... "

Bidwell: "After six months we had now arrived at the first settlement in California, November 4, 1841. Dr. Marsh's ranch [Dr. John Marsh, who had arrived in 1836] was located in the eastern foothills of the Coast Range Mountains, near the northwestern extremity of the great San Joaquin Valley and about eight miles east of Mount Diablo. There were no other settlements in the valley; it was, apparently, still just as new as when Columbus discovered America, and roaming over it were countless thousands of wild horses, of elk, and of antelopes."

California exceeded John Bidwell's expectations in every regard. Among the first audacious Americans to emigrate to California, Bidwell was also one of the first to strike it rich. Very rich. With a fortune acquired after finding gold on the Feather River, he purchased 24,000 acres on the future site of Chico. Bidwell became prominent in politics, served in Congress, and in 1892, made a run for the presidency as the candidate of the Prohibition Party. Dawson remained in California less than three years and, after further travels, settled in Austin, Texas.

Slowly, migration to central California had begun and would continue, although it diminished, even during the War with Mexico, from 1846 to February, 1848. Nothing could stop Americans from coming. And when word spread about James Marshall's discovery of gold at Sutter's Mill (which had happened just two weeks before the end of the war), California became a mecca for fortune-seekers not only from the American settlements but from all over the world. The gold rush of '49 brought on a flood of settlers, a flood that has not ceased to this day: California's population is the largest of the nation's fifty states.

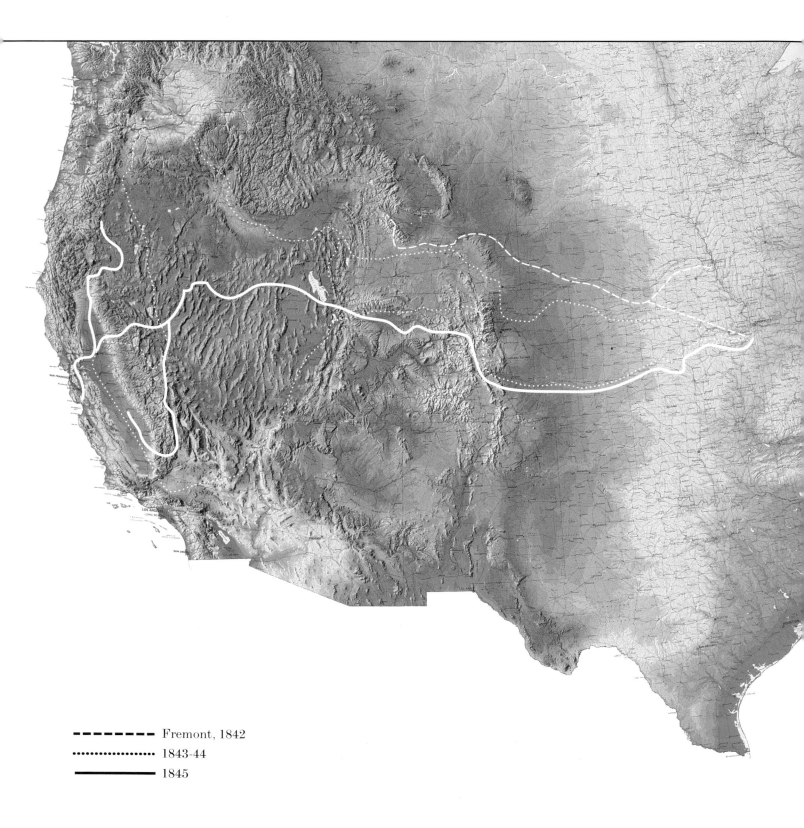

Fremont, 1842
1843-44
1845

The narration in this chapter derives from Frémont's A Report of the Exploring Expedition to Oregon and North California in the Years 1843-44, *submitted to Colonel John J. Abert, chief of the Corps of Topographical Engineers, as edited in 1970 by the preeminent historians Donald Jackson and Mary Lee Spence.*

Chapter 16

MANIFEST DESTINY: FREMONT'S SANTA FE EXPEDITION

While the first overland emigrant party to California was struggling across the Great Basin and over the Sierras, another party was making its way from Austin, Texas, to Santa Fe, New Mexico. The Santa Fe Expedition had as one of its presumptuous goals the annexation of that portion of the Mexican province of New Mexico lying east of the Rio Grande River. Their disastrous crusade, which led the party through the Palo Duro Canyon and across the Tucumcari Mountains in New Mexico, was capped by the survivors' capture and imprisonment by the Mexicans, in some cases their torture and execution, and a two-thousand-mile forced march to Mexico City. Those who made it were ultimately released by order of General Santa Anna, president of Mexico.

A series of conflicts with Mexico, initiated by the Mexicans in retaliation for the Santa Fe Expedition, then ensued. By mid-May 1846, the United States and Mexico were at war.

Many factors had created tensions between Mexico and the United States. The most cogent, however, was the emergence of a compelling notion that it was America's destiny, as expressed by an editorial writer, "to overspread and possess the whole of the continent which Providence has given us for the development of the great experiment of liberty and federated self-government."

The United States' era of conscious "manifest destiny" had begun in 1842, although the phrase itself did not come into use until 1845. President John Tyler, influenced by the ardent expansionist senator from Missouri, Thomas Hart Benton, authorized Benton's son-in-law, John Charles Frémont, to lead an expedition along the Oregon Trail to the South Pass "in aid of and auxiliary to the Oregon Emigration." Frémont, a controversial character in United States history, was instructed to write a report on travel conditions, to prepare a map of the route, and to recommend locations for the erection of military forts from which the Army could protect the emigrants.

Frémont's 1842 expedition on the Oregon Trail, guided by Kit Carson, contained only two notable moments: his ascent of a peak in the Wind River Mountains, which now bears his name, and his attempt to navigate the Sweetwater River, which ended in near-disaster when his bull-boat capsized in turbulent rapids.

Frémont's 1843 expedition to survey from the South Pass to the Pacific Northwest, however, was an epic journey. Frémont's party of thirty-nine included several men who had been on his first expedition. Thomas Fitzpatrick served as his guide, with Jim Bridger and another famous mountain-man, Alexis Godey, joining the expedition when it reached the Rockies. Charles Preuss, from Germany, was the party's cartographer.

"To make the exploration as useful as possible," Frémont wrote, "I determined to vary the route to the Rocky mountains from that followed in the year 1842. The route then was up the valley of the Great Platte river to the South Pass; the route now determined on was up the valley of the Kansas river, and to the head of the Arkansas, and to some pass in the mountains, if any could be found, at the sources of that river."

The expedition departed on May 29 from "the little town of Kansas on the Missouri frontier, near the junction of the Kansas river with the Missouri." As Frémont rode westward, "trains of wagons were almost constantly in sight, giving the road a populous and animated appearance." The emigrants were cheered at seeing Frémont on the trail, an official symbol of the new attitude of the United States.

On the way to Fort St. Vrain on the South Platte (south of today's Greeley, Colorado), Frémont came to a fork of the Republican River, in an area "populous with prairie dogs," and "gave to this stream the name of Prairie Dog River." Beyond Fort St. Vrain, Frémont headed southward along the foot of the Rockies, seeking an alternate to South Pass, until he came to a small farming community on the Arkansas River established by several mountaineers with their Mexican wives, the site of Pueblo, Colorado. Here Kit Carson joined Frémont, and they returned to Fort St. Vrain, still seeking a pass to the west.

South Pass would continue for many years to be the emigrant passage through the Rockies, and this is where Frémont now headed to rejoin the Oregon Trail. He made an encampment on the springs at the foot of Pike's Peak, today's Manitou Springs near Colorado Springs, "all the people being anxious to drink of these famous waters."

At Fort St. Vrain, Frémont separated his party "into two divisions, one of which, under the command of Mr. Fitzpatrick, was directed to cross the plains to the mouth of the Laramie river, and continuing thence its route along the usual emigrant road [the Oregon Trail, and] meet me at Fort Hall ..." Frémont, accompanied by Kit Carson, led the smaller party northwestward across the Medicine Bow Mountains [in Wyoming], "having determined to try the passage by a pass through a spur of the mountains made by the Cache-la-Poudre river." When he reached the Oregon Trail at the confluence of the Sweetwater and the North Platte rivers (future site of the Pathfinder Dam, named in Frémont's honor), he noted that the party was encamped on the "river endeared to us by the acquaintance of the previous expedition.

"Here passes the road to Oregon; and the broad smooth highway, where the numerous heavy wagons of the emigrants had entirely beaten and crushed the artemisia [sagebrush], was a happy exchange to our poor animals for the sharp rocks and tough shrubs among which they had been toiling so long; and we moved up the valley rapidly and pleasantly." Frémont then followed the trail to the "fertile and picturesque valley of Bear River" in Idaho.

"Crossing, in the afternoon, the point of a narrow spur, we descended into a beautiful bottom, formed by a lateral valley, which presented a picture of home beauty that went directly to our hearts. The edge of the wood, for several miles along the river, was dotted

PIKE'S PEAK

179

with the white covers of emigrant wagons, collected in groups at different camps, where the smokes were rising lazily from the fires, around which women were occupied in preparing the evening meal, and the children playing in the grass; and herds of cattle, grazing about in the bottom, had an air of quiet security and civilized comfort that made a rare sight for the traveller in such a remote wilderness."

(Frémont had come upon the "Great Emigration" of 1843, close to one thousand settlers trekking to Oregon with some two thousand head of cattle. This romantically described sojourn of the emigrants in the valley of the Bear River was a rare respite from an otherwise difficult journey.)

Frémont next turned to "one of the main objectives contemplated in the general plan of our survey—an examination of the great lake which is the outlet of this river ... " He claimed that his reconnaissance of the Great Salt Lake would be "the first ever attempted on this interior sea," but he might have been unaware that in the spring of 1826 the lake's western shore had been explored by a party dispatched by Jedediah Strong Smith.

Great Salt Lake

From Little Mountain, west of today's Ogden, Utah, Frémont first "beheld the object of our anxious search—the waters of the Inland Sea, stretching in still and solitary grandeur far beyond the limit of our vision. It was one of the great points of the exploration; and as we looked eagerly over the lake in the first emotions of excited pleasure, I am doubtful if the followers of Balboa felt more enthusiasm when, from the height of the Andes, they saw for the first time the great Western ocean … to travellers so long shut up among mountain ranges, a sudden view over the expanse of silent waters had in it something sublime. Several large islands raised their high rocky heads out of the waves."

LITTLE BEAR RIVER, UTAH

In an "India-rubber boat, 18 feet long," Frémont, Kit Carson, Charles Preuss, and two other men pushed off from the southeastern shore of the Great Salt Lake, and spent a night camping on a barren island near today's Antelope Island, which Frémont named. "The cliffs and masses of rock along the shore were whitened by an incrustation of salt where the waves dashed up against them; and the evaporating water, which had been left in holes and hollows on the surface of the rocks, was covered with a crust of salt about one-eighth of an inch in thickness." Frémont named the rocky island "Disappointment."

Back on shore, Frémont reascended Bear River. "The bottoms of this river and some of the creeks which I saw form a natural resting and recruiting station for travellers, now, and in all time to come. The bottoms are extensive; water excellent; timber sufficient; the soil good and well adapted to the grains and grasses suited to such an elevated region. A military post, and a civilized settlement, would be of great value here; and cattle and horses would do well where grass and salt so much abound." He described it as "truly a bucolic region."

Beyond Fort Hall, Frémont proceeded along the Oregon Trail, coming to the "missionary establishment of Dr. Whitman" on the Walla Walla River. From the mission the party went on to nearby Fort Walla Walla, where "we saw for the first time the great river [the Columbia] on which the course of events for the last half century had been directing attention and conferring historical fame. The river is, indeed, a noble object, and has here attained its full magnitude."

Fort Vancouver, where the travelers were greeted by the remarkable John McLoughlin, had become the joyous terminal point for emigrants on the Oregon Trail. Frémont's official survey was now completed.

Frémont noted: "The camp was occupied in making the necessary preparations for our homeward journey, which, though homeward, contemplated a new route, and a great circuit to the south and southeast, and the exploration of the Great Basin between the Rocky Mountains and the Sierra Nevada." (Frémont was first to recognize and name the Great Basin.) Another of his objectives in making the long detour was to determine the location of a mysterious river that had long been presumed to exist, and which even appeared on some early maps, but which had never been seen. It was known as the Buenaventura and was believed to flow "from the Rocky mountains to the bay of San Francisco."

MOUNT HOOD

At the beginning of winter a party of twenty-five returned to the Dalles, and from there headed southward along the Des Chutes River. "We had a grand view of St. Helens and Regnier [Rainier]." St. Helens had erupted the year before, and "had scattered its ashes, like a light fall of snow, over the Dalles of the Columbia, 50 miles distant." Frémont also "had a fine view of Mount Hood, a rose-colored mass of snow." He noted that "in all our journeying, we had never travelled through a country where the rivers were so abounding in falls, and the name of this stream [the Des Chutes] is singularly characteristic. At every place where we come in the neighborhood of the river is heard the roaring of falls."

After reaching Klamath Marsh, "the further continuation of our voyage assumed a character of discovery and exploration . . .

"Passing the mountains of what is today the Frémont National Forest, Frémont came to a large lake which he named Abert "in honor of the chief of the corps to which I belonged." He then headed southward (into Nevada) and at the edge of Black Rock Desert "concluded the year 1843, and our new year's eve was rather a gloomy one. The result of our journey began to be very uncertain; the country was singularly unfavorable to travel"—even now there are only a few dirt and gravel roads in this section of northwest Nevada—"the grasses being of a very unwholesome character, and the hoofs of our animals were so worn and cut by the rocks that many of them were lame and could scarcely be got along.

"Our situation had now become a serious one. The appearance of the country was so forbidding that I was afraid to enter it, and determined to bear away to the southward, keeping close along the mountains, in the full expectation of reaching the Buenaventura river." Struggling southward, the party came to a lake from which rose a remarkable six-hundred-foot-high rock "presenting a pretty exact outline of the great pyramid of Cheops. This striking feature suggested a name for the lake; and I called it Pyramid Lake."

THE SIERRA NEVADA MOUNTAINS FROM THE EAST

At the Truckee River (east of today's Reno), Frémont decided "to abandon my eastern course and to cross the Sierra Nevada into the valley of the Sacramento, wherever a practicable pass could be found. My decision was heard with joy by the people and diffused new life throughout the camp."

Crossing the Sierra Nevada Range at this time of year, late January, would be a formidable task. "The mountains were darkened with fallen snow, and, feeling unwilling to encounter them, we turned to the southward." On the Walker River, a young Indian guide was engaged to lead the party across the mountains.

Frémont gathered his men and told them that over the mountains "almost directly west, and only about 70 miles distant, was the great farming establishment of Captain Sutter."

Even had he been right about the seventy-mile estimate, what lay between the men and the sanctuary of Sutter's Fort were the demanding ascents and descents of the snow-covered peaks of the central range. On the morning of February 2, when, temporarily, "it had ceased snowing," Frémont led his men into the Sierra Nevadas. "The people were unusually silent; for every man knew that our enterprise was hazardous, and the issue doubtful."

On the slopes of the first ascent they occasionally passed "low huts entirely covered with snow," in which Indians were huddled for survival. An old Indian warned them to retreat and seek a better way through the mountains. "'Rock upon rock, rock upon rock, snow upon snow, snow upon snow,' said he. 'Even if you get over the snow, you will not be able to get down from the mountains.'" When their young Indian guide heard this alarming warning, he suddenly disappeared, but Frémont and his men proceeded without him.

"The glare of the snow, combined with great fatigue, rendered many of the people nearly blind; but we were fortunate in having some black silk handkerchiefs which, worn as veils, very much relieved the eye." After two weeks of hardship they reached a pass "in the dividing ridge of the Sierra," where Frémont climbed a peak and "had a beautiful view of a mountain lake at our feet, about fifteen miles in length, and so entirely surrounded by mountains that we could not discover an outlet." It was Lake Tahoe.

Finally, a month after they had entered the mountains, they emerged into the valley of the American River, "Rio de los Americanos," and moving in small detachments, straggled into Sutter's Fort. When Tom Fitzpatrick's detachment, which had been bringing up the rear, arrived at the fort, "a more forlorn and pitiable sight than they presented cannot well be imagined."

After "repose and enjoyment" at Sutter's Fort, the expedition started its homeward journey. "Our direct course home was east, but the Sierra would force us south, about five hundred miles of travelling, to a pass at the head of the San Joaquin river. To reach it, our course lay along the valley of the San Joaquin, the river on our right and the lofty wall of the impassable Sierra on our left."

Lake Tahoe, photographed at the same time of year Fremont first saw it

Marching in the valley, "it was pleasant, riding among this assemblage of green pastures with varied flowers and scattered groves, and out of the warm, green spring to look at the rocky and snowy peaks where lately we had suffered so much." North of today's Mojave, Frémont turned eastward and crossed the mountains via a pass near Tehachapi, descending from California into the Great Basin.

"We here left the waters of the bay of San Francisco, and, though forced upon them contrary to my intentions I cannot regret the necessity which occasioned the deviation. It made me well acquainted with the great range of the Sierra Nevada of the Alta California, and showed that this broad and elevated snowy ridge was a continuation of the Cascade Range of Oregon, between which and the ocean there is still another and a lower range, parallel to the former and to the coast, and which may be called the Coast Range. It also made me well acquainted with the basin of the San Francisco bay, and cleared up some points in geography on which error had long prevailed." One of them was the supposed existence of the Buenaventura River.

An Indian who had guided the party to the Great Basin now stretched out his hand and said, "'There the great "llanos," plains;"no hay agua; no hay zavate—nada": there is neither water nor grass, nothing; every animal that goes out upon them dies.' It was indeed dismal to look upon, and hard to conceive so great a change in so short a distance. One might travel the world over without finding a valley more fresh and verdant, more floral and sylvan, more alive with birds and animals, more bounteously watered than we had left in the San Joaquin; here, within a few miles ride, a vast desert plain spread before us, from which the boldest traveller turned away in despair."

The Great Basin lay ahead, but now the men were ready for it. They had good horses, strong mules and plentiful supplies. They felt refreshed and reinvigorated after their sojourn at Sutter's Fort and their pleasant journey in the San Joaquin Valley. Turning southward to avoid the Mojave Desert, they struck the Old Spanish Trail, a trade route connecting Los Angeles with Santa Fe. (Too difficult for wagon travel, it never became an emigrant trail.)

The party proceeded to a camping ground called "'las vegas,' a term which the Spaniards use to signify fertile or marshy plains, in contradistinction to 'llanos,' which they apply to dry and sterile plains." From the future site of the glittering gamblers' city of Las Vegas, the men made their way through a stretch of "between fifty and sixty miles without a drop of water, where the heated air seemed to be entirely deprived of moisture." When they reached Muddy River, they were harassed by Southern Paiute Indians and followed for several days, as the party moved along the Virgin River.

At last out of the desert, at Santa Clara in the southwest corner of Utah, the party came to a well-known resting place on the Old Spanish Trail. (This spot, then known as Mountain Meadows, was the site in 1857 of the massacre of 120 emigrants by a band of fanatic Mormons.) Here they "had the gratification to be joined by the famous hunter and trapper, Mr. Joseph Walker." The discoverer of Yosemite had been accompanying a trader's caravan from California some distance behind, and seeing the tracks of what he presumed to be the

CAPITAL REEF NATIONAL PARK IN UTAH

Frémont party, had hurried ahead to overtake it. Walker was familiar with the route, and took over guidance of the party on its way from the Old Spanish Trail northward through spectacular Utah terrain (traversing, some believe, Zion National Park) to the valley of the Sevier, and up to Utah Lake and the Wasatch Range. There Fitzpatrick and Carson again took over as the party proceeded eastward, through terrain familiar to the two veteran mountain men, to Brown's Hole on the Green River and then to a point south of South Pass.

From here Frémont turned his party "southwardly [where] there were objects worthy to be explored." The party journeyed from Wyoming into Colorado. He explored "New Park," now known as North Park, came to what was then known as the Grand River (later acknowledged to be the origin of the Colorado River, and was so named, in Middle Park), and after traversing Bayou Salade, South Park, went past Pueblo to Bent's Fort on the Arkansas River (east of La Junta).

The expedition arrived at St. Louis on August 7, 1844. Frémont's widely read *Reports*, with their romantic descriptions of the Oregon Trail and the Rocky Mountains, induced many families to emigrate to the West—precisely what Thomas Hart Benton, the expedition's sponsor, had had in mind. The excellent maps prepared by Charles Preuss, especially of the Oregon Trail, were so detailed and accurate that emigrant parties could make the trek even without experienced guides.

And make the trek they did, in ever increasing numbers, with and without guides. The Great Emigration of 1843 was exceeded in numbers of westering families by those of 1844 and 1845.

Frémont became a national hero, and was dubbed "the Pathfinder." Though he was later convicted by court-martial for his behavior during the Mexican War, and censured by President Abraham Lincoln for his conduct in the Civil War, Frémont's expeditions had served his country well.

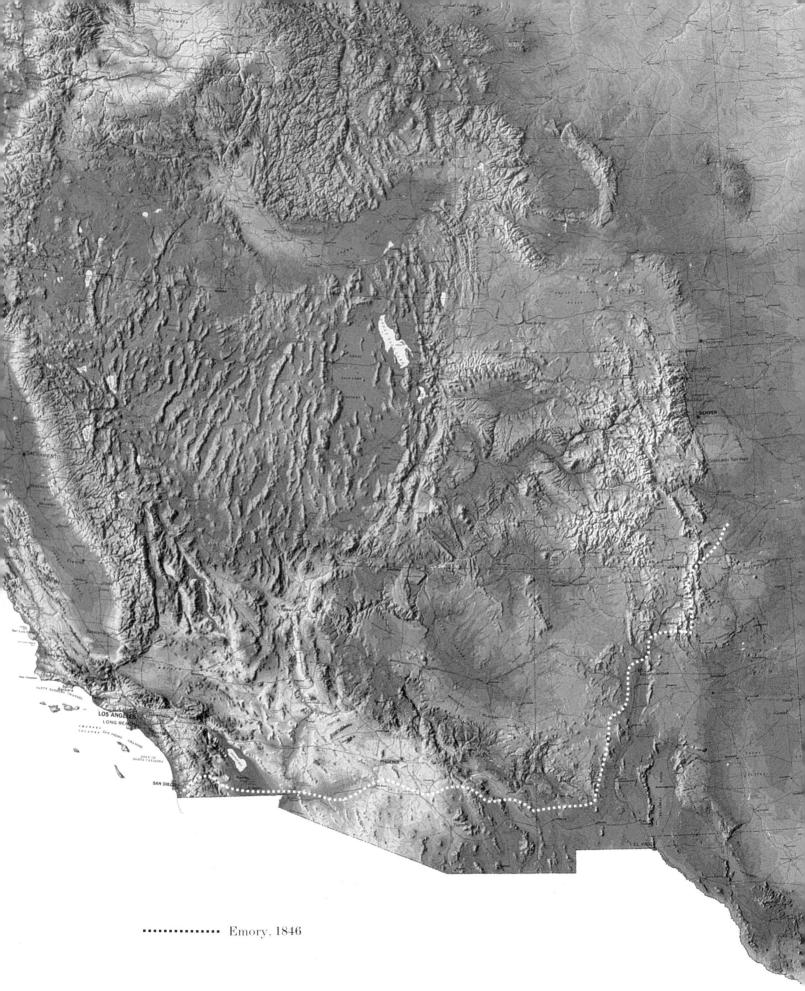

·············· Emory, 1846

Lieutenant Emory's Notes of a Military Reconnaissance *narrates not only Kearny's encounters with the Mexican forces, but also Emory's important first-time explorations of ancient sites in New Mexico and Arizona.*

Chapter 17

WILLIAM EMORY AND THE ARMY OF THE WEST

Less than a month after war with Mexico had been officially declared by President James Polk, Lieutenant William Emory, Maryland gentleman, scholar and scientist, explorer and soldier, entered the saga of the West as the official reporter of the march of the Army of the West and the surveys of the topographical engineers assigned to its commander, Stephen Kearny.

The date was June 5. The year was 1846. It was the year in which the dispute with England over possession of the Oregon Country was settled peaceably through diplomatic negotiation. It was also the year in which the dispute with Mexico over the annexation of Texas erupted into a multi-front war.

The Army of the West, in addition to six companies of Kearny's regiment, the First Dragoons, included eight companies of the First Missouri volunteers, the Laclede rangers, a troop of cavalry from St. Louis, and Emory's detachment of topographical engineers. The Army was trailed to Santa Fe, for the protection which it provided, by a large caravan of traders, consisting of more than fifteen hundred wagons and twenty thousand oxen, cattle, mules, and horses.

"The route of Colonel Kearny's command," Emory wrote, "would be through unexplored regions [requiring that] the attention of myself and the officers assigned to duty with me, should be employed in collecting data which would give the government some idea of the regions. The country between Fort Leavenworth and Santa Fe, traversed by the Army of the West, may be divided into three great divisions, distinct in character, climate, and products, viz: from Fort Leavenworth to Pawnee Fork, from Pawnee Fork to Bent's Fort, and from Bent's Fort to Santa Fe. The first two divisions have been so often traversed that I have omitted my diary embracing them." The third was in large part an unfamiliar region.

The terrain beyond Bent's Fort in southeastern Colorado, from which the Army departed in early August, was arid and parched. "The pasture was so bad that Colonel Kearny determined to march to the 'hole in the prairie' where grass and water were available." It was a welcome respite on the way to New Mexico. At the Vermijo River, after crossing rugged, twisting Raton Pass, "five Mexicans were captured by [William] Bent's spy company."

As the troops approached the town of Las Vegas (New Mexico), "information was received that 600 men had collected at the pass which debouches into the Vegas, two miles distant, and were to oppose our march." From the rooftop of an adobe house, Kearny, who had just been commissioned as brigadier general, told the inhabitants of the town that the United States considered it part of its territory, their allegiance to the Mexican government was absolved, and they would be protected if they remained peaceably at home and hanged if they did not. The Army of the West continued on its way, unopposed, to the town of Pecos.

What Emory did next earns him the distinction of having been the first to study the archaeology of the Southwest. A man of broad scientific pursuits—botany, astronomy, topography, geology—he was now fascinated by the archaeology of the ancient Indian settlements, many of which he was to see on this expedition, and the first of which were the Pecos ruins (now Pecos National Monument). This was the site of an Indian Pueblo where "the remains of the architecture exhibit, in a prominent manner, the engraftment of the Catholic church upon the ancient religion of the country. Two religions so entirely different

THE RUINS OF PECOS

in theory were here, as in all Mexico, blended in harmonious practice until about a century since when the town was sacked by a band of Indians" (the Pueblo Rebellion of 1680).

The road was clear "between the army and Santa Fe, the capital of New Mexico." The march was made in one day and the United States flag raised "over the palace before sundown."

Emory observed: "The houses are of mud bricks, in the Spanish style, generally of one story, and built on a square. The interior of the square is an open court, and the principal rooms open into it. They are forbidding in appearance from the outside, but nothing can exceed the comfort and convenience of the interior. The thick walls make them cool in summer and warm in winter."

Late in September the First Dragoons, led by Kearny, descended the Rio Grande beyond Albuquerque. South of Socorro the troops turned westward to head for the Gila River. Emory noted that he "longed to cross the mountains [Los Pintos, to the east] and explore the haunts of the Apaches and the hiding places of the Comanches [but] we were not an exploring expedition; war was the object; yet we had now marched one thousand miles without flashing a sabre."

On October 6, Kit Carson rode into camp with a small detachment from California, "bearing intelligence that that country had surrendered without a blow, and that the American flag floated in every port."

Striking out for the Mimbres Mountains, General Kearny found the terrain so broken that he decided to send the wagons back and proceed with pack mules. After a slow, difficult stretch of mountain travel the expedition came to the Gila River, which rises in the Mogollon Mountains in southwest New Mexico.

In today's Gila Wilderness Area, the expedition reached "the ground where rumor and the maps of the day place the ruins of the so-called Aztec towns." Emory found hieroglyphics, "unknown characters written on a rock." He examined "one of the long-sought ruins minutely, and the only evidence of handicraft remaining were immense quantities of broken pottery, extending for miles along the river." In the cliffs he found "what must have been at times the abodes of the Indians and the dens of beasts. The remains of fire and the bones of animals attested this." He had time to make only a superficial archaeological dig, and a few feet under the surface he came to "a solid mass which was most likely a dirt floor, as is now used by the Spanish." (This was the first reported exploration of present-day Gila Cliff Dwellings National Monument.)

The Army of the West would now follow the Gila River westward to California. This important river of the Southwest goes through an ever-changing terrain on its descent to the Colorado. In the mountains of New Mexico it is a fast-running, clear mountain stream bordered by pines and aspens. As it descends into Arizona and winds its way toward Phoenix, it flows through arid, semi-desert country.

As Emory noted, "the road before us was unknown." When the troops entered today's Arizona, they came to a section of the Gila that Kit Carson had traversed on his way from California. Carson told them that it was difficult and dangerous, and should now be avoided if possible. However, there was "no alternative but to pursue Carson's old trail sixty miles over a rough country, without water, and two, if not three days' journey." Spaniards knew this stretch (at the foot of the Gila Mountains in Arizona) as a *jornada del muerte,* a journey of death. Emory observed that "the only animals seen were lizards, scorpions, and tarantulas. The [giant saguaro] and every other variety of cactus flourished in great luxuriance. The [saguaro], tall, erect, and columnar in its appearance"—one, said Emory, was fifty feet tall— "grew in every crevice from the base to the top of the mountains. These extraordinary looking plants seem to seek the wildest and most unfrequented space."

Coming through the gorge of the Gila, Emory found it "gullied on each side by deep and impassable *arroyos*"; the soldiers named it "the Devil's Turnpike." At the confluence of the Gila with the San Carlos River (now the site of Coolidge Dam), Emory found another ancient settlement in ruins, seeing such an immense assortment of shards that he concluded they must have been pieces of irrigation pipes built by the prehistoric Indians. (These ruins are now under the waters of the reservoir.)

At the junction of the Gila with the Salt River, the Army of the West came to the lands of the Pima, Papago, and Maricopa, where Emory admired "the beauty, order, and disposition of the arrangements for irrigating and draining the land. Corn, wheat, and cotton are the crops . . ."

One of the Papagos guided Emory to what the Indians called "Casa Montezuma" (today's Casa Grande Ruins National Monument). "The Casa was in complete ruins, one pile of broken pottery and foundation stone, of the black basalt, making a mound about ten feet above the ground. The outline of the ground plan was distinct enough." Emory found seashells also, leading him to infer that these Indians traveled to or traded with the Indians of the Pacific, and "a large bead, an inch and a quarter in length, of bluish marble, exquisitely turned"—the first mention in any of the chronicles of the ubiquitous ornamental stone of the Indian Southwest, the turquoise.

THE GILA RIVER IN ARIZONA

Continuing westward along the Gila, Emory came to the big bend of the river, where he found rocks "covered with unknown characters; the work of human hands. One stone bore on it what might be taken with a little stretch of the imagination, to be a mastodon, a horse, a dog, and a man. Some of the boulders appear to have been written and re-written upon so often it was impossible to get a distinct outline of any of the characters." (Reproductions of the petroglyphics are included in Emory's *Notes*, along with wonderful sketches of various landmarks by J. M. Stanley—many originals of which were destroyed in a fire at the Smithsonian—and topographical sketches by Lt. W. H. Warner and Lt. G. W. Peck; and a valuable map, first of the area, which resulted from Emory's painstaking daily surveying efforts.)

As the column approached the Colorado River (at Yuma, Arizona), "the day was warm, the dust oppressive, and the march, twenty-two miles, very long for our jaded and ill-fed brutes." The Army of the West forded the Colorado and headed into "the great desert of drifting sands" (beyond Winterhaven, California, on the Arizona border). As they plodded on, Emory wrote: "We are still to look for the glowing pictures drawn of California. As yet, barrenness and desolation hold reign." (Many years later this area was to become the fertile Imperial Valley.)

Beyond the desert lay the Santa Rosa Mountains and beyond them the Agua Caliente Valley, site of Jonathan Warner's Ranch (which was to become an arrival station for emigrants bound for Southern California, serving a role similar to that of Sutter's Ranch in Northern California).

On December 6, 1846, the Army of the West had its first military engagement with the Mexicans and suffered heavy losses. The Mexicans fled, however, upon the arrival of reinforcements and the Army encountered no further resistance in its march to San Diego. From the summit of a hill, "the Pacific opened for the first time in our view, the sight producing strange but agreeable emotions. One of the mountain men who had never seen the ocean before, opened his arms and exclaimed, 'Lord! there is a great prairie without a tree!' "

The war with Mexico came to an official end on all fronts with the signing on February 2, 1848, of the treaty of Guadalupe Hidalgo, which brought under American dominion an area as immense as that acquired in 1803 with the Louisiana Territory. It includes present-day California, New Mexico, Texas, Utah, Nevada, most of Arizona, the Oklahoma Panhandle, most of Colorado, southwestern Kansas, and southwestern Wyoming.

It was the year when gold was discovered in California. It was also the year John Jacob Astor died, at the age of eighty-four.

America's "manifest destiny" had been realized. The entire West, south of the 49th parallel and north of today's border with Mexico, was now in the possession of the United States. Much of it was still unexplored.

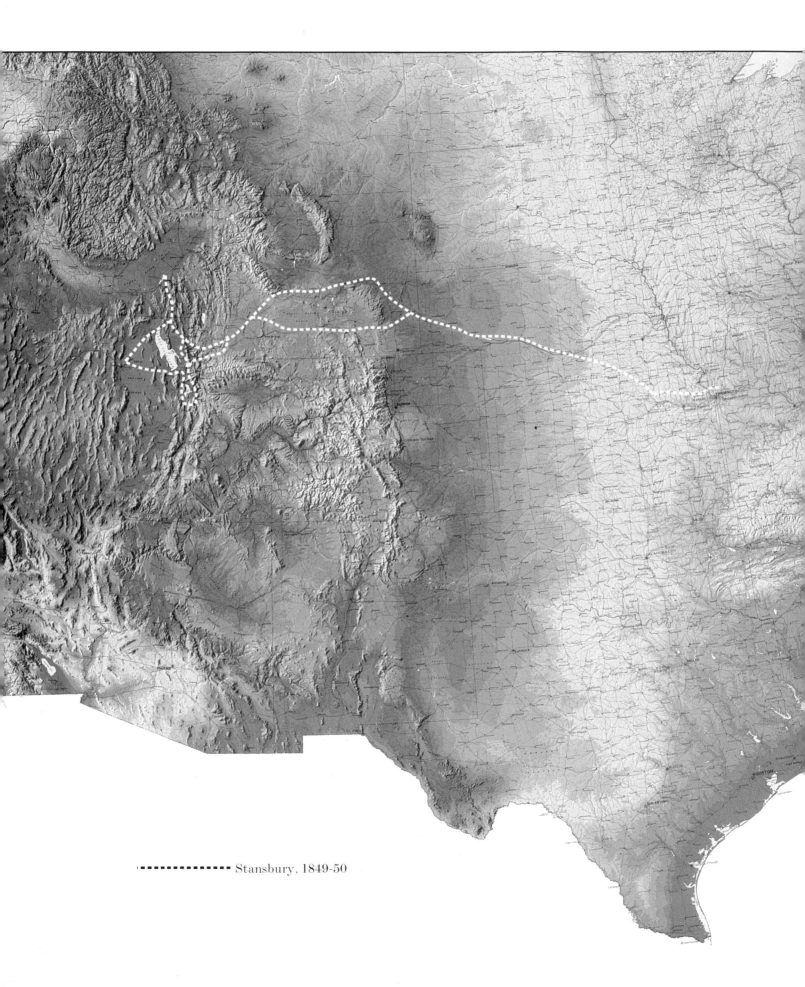

Stansbury, 1849-50

Published as a Senate Executive Document, Stansbury's journals were entitled Exploration and Survey of the Valley of the Great Salt Lake of Utah.
Other material is taken from Frederick Turner, historian of the western frontier, in The Frontier in American History.

Chapter 18

HOWARD STANSBURY:
EXPLORING THE UTAH BASIN AND THE GREAT SALT LAKE

After the U.S. acquisition of much of the Southwest in 1848, it was apparent that the westering emigrants, and those attracted to the California gold fields, would need military protection along the trails, that new and better trails would have to be blazed, and that routes for railroad lines to the Pacific would have to be surveyed. There was a need to have this *terra incognita* officially and properly explored and surveyed.

This task was assigned to the Corps of Topographical Engineers of the United States Army, which had already benefited from the successful work of Frémont and William Emory.

Of the many significant expeditions in 1849, one of the most was that led by Captain Howard Stansbury under instructions to reconnoiter the Platte River trail, the country west of it across the Wasatch Mountains, the Utah Basin, the Great Salt Lake, and to report on the Mormon settlements in and near Salt Lake City. The expedition departed from Fort Leavenworth, Kansas, May 31, 1849, consisting "of eighteen men, five wagons, and forty-six horses and mules." The route taken by the party had already been traveled by thousands of people. Through June, as the expedition proceeded, Stansbury encountered many sad evidences of the hardships endured by the emigrants.

The expedition encamped near Fort Kearny, recently constructed at the site of Nebraska City, where commanding officer Benjamin Bonneville, "whose adventures among the Rocky Mountains are so well known to the world, . . . received us very courteously, offering us every facility in his power in furtherance of our progress."

On the way to Fort Laramie, Stansbury came across one of the commercial enterprises which were beginning to appear along the Oregon Trail—a blacksmith who had set up shop at Scott's Bluff to serve the emigration. At a ford of the North Platte, beyond Deer Creek, he came across another commercial enterprise—a crude ferry charging two dollars per wagon.

Near the Red Buttes in the Laramie Mountains, there was again "evidence of the difficulties encountered by those who are ahead of us. The road has been literally strewn with articles that have been thrown away. Bar-iron and steel, large blacksmiths' anvils and bellows, cross-bars, drills, augers, gold-washers, chisels, axes, lead, trucks, spades, ploughs, large grind-stones, baking-ovens, cooking-stoves, kegs, barrels, harness, clothing, bacon, and beans, were found along the road in pretty much the order in which they have been here enumerated. In the course of this one day the relics of seventeen wagons and the carcasses of twenty-seven dead oxen have been seen."

The expedition came to Fort Bridger on Blacks' Fork of the Green River and was received "with great kindness and lavish hospitality by the proprietor, Major James Bridger." From Fort Bridger, Stansbury turned southward to search for a possible wagon road across the Wasatch Mountains to Salt Lake City. Jim Bridger served as guide, and they found a good route that was subsequently chosen for a railroad line.

At Salt Lake City, Stansbury called upon Brigham Young and the newly settled Mormons who, persuaded by Stansbury that "no evil was intended to his people," offered their assistance in the survey.

Before undertaking the exploration of the Great Salt Lake, Stansbury left Salt Lake City "to . . . explore a route for a road from the head of Salt Lake to Fort Hall." While the survey of Utah Lake commenced, Stansbury succeeded in tracing an "excellent wagon-road" between Salt Lake and Fort Hall, two important sites on the emigrant trail to California.

In late October, he made "preparations for an exploration of the desert terrain on the western shore of the lake." Old mountain-men warned Stansbury that the "reconnaissance was not only hazardous in the highest degree, but absolutely impracticable, especially at so late a season of the year." Indians warned him that water would be "extremely scarce and the country destitute of game."

The party set off, and first encountered the Promontory Mountains in the northeast section of the Great Salt Lake. The survey of the areas to the north and west of the lake, in the Great Salt Lake Desert, proved to be as difficult as Stansbury had been warned it would be. At one point he feared that the mules might give out from lack of water and forage, "in which case we must perish in the wilderness." Of the barren salt flats he wrote: "So firm and strong

THE GREAT SALT LAKE DESERT

was this unique and snowy floor that it sustained the weight of our entire train without in the least giving way or cracking under the pressure. Our mules walked upon it as upon a sheet of solid ice." (The party was not far from today's Bonneville Speedway.)

At one point, when Stansbury was "doubtful whether even the best mule we had could have gone more than a half dozen miles farther, we beheld to our infinite joy a small prairie or meadow covered with a profusion of good green grass, through which meandered a small stream of pure fresh running water. Another day without water and the whole train must have inevitably perished. Both man and beast being completely exhausted, I remained here three days for refreshment and rest. Moreover, we were now to prepare for crossing another desert of seventy miles, which, as my guide informed me, still lay between us and the southern end of the lake. He had passed over it in 1845, with Frémont [on his third western expedition], who had lost ten mules and several horses in effecting this passage, having afterward encamped on the same ground now occupied by our little party." Approaching the south shore of the lake, Stansbury came to today's Temple Springs, where there were "several large springs of excellent water . . .

"The route from the Salt Lake to this point was first taken by Colonel Frémont, in 1845. A year afterwards, it was followed by a party of emigrants [the Donner Party] under a Mr. Hastings, whence its present name of 'Hastings Cut-off.' A portion of his company which had followed at some distance behind him, becoming belated in crossing the Sierra Nevada Mountains, a number of them perished, and the remainder were reduced to the revolting necessity of living upon the bodies of their dead comrades, until they were rescued by relief from Sutter's Fort."

Stansbury described part of the terrain the Hastings Cut-off, soon abandoned, which he had crossed: "The western shore of the lake is bounded by an immense level plain consisting of soft mud, frequently traversed by small, meandering rills of salt and sulphurous water, with occasional springs of fresh, all of which sink before reaching the lake. These streams seem to imbue and saturate the whole soil so as to render it throughout miry and treacherous. For a few months, in midsummer, the sun has sufficient influence to render some portions of the plain, for a short time, dry and hard; in these intervals the travelling over it is excellent, but one heavy shower is sufficient to reconvert the hardened clay into soft, tenacious mud, rendering the passage of teams over it toilsome, and frequently quite hazardous."

Stansbury returned to Salt Lake City. "The winter season in the valley was long and severe. The vicinity of so many high mountains rendered the weather extremely variable; snows constantly fell upon them, and frequently to the depth of fifty feet, filling up the passes so rapidly that, in more than one instance, emigrants who had been belated in starting from

the States were overtaken by the storms in the mountain gorges, and forced to abandon everything and escape on foot, leaving even their animals to perish in the snows."

Stansbury spent the winter among the Mormons. With the advent of spring, he set out for his "critical examination of this interesting area and hitherto almost unknown region, and the remarkable body of water to which it is indebted for the interest which attaches to it."

The boat party embarked on the Jordan River, which links Utah Lake with Great Salt Lake, while the shore party proceeded to the southern rim. From Antelope Island Stansbury's party boated to what the Mormons called Castle Island, which Frémont had called Disappointment Island. Stansbury renamed it Frémont Island.

For three months Stansbury and his men worked on their survey of the lake. On an island which he named Gunnison's Island in honor of his esteemed aide, Stansbury saw "immense flocks of pelicans and gulls, disturbed now for the first time probably by the intrusion of man." Another island was named after Stansbury, "a large island west of Antelope Island, which the officers of the party had done me the honor to call by my name."

Late in August, having successfully completed his important assignment, Captain Stansbury headed his expedition homeward. But there was yet more that he wanted to accomplish. "Before leaving Salt Lake Valley, it had been determined not to return by the beaten track, but to endeavor to ascertain the practicability of some more direct route that now travelled

AN UNMARKED GRAVE ON THE OREGON TRAIL

to the waters of the Atlantic [across the Continental Divide]. If it should prove to be practicable to carry a road across the North Fork of the Platte, near the Medicine Bow Butte, and skirting the southern limits of the Laramie Plains, to cross the Black Hills [Laramie Mountains] in the vicinity of Lodge-Pole Creek, and to descent the stream to its junction with the South Fork of the Platte, nearly a straight line would thus be accomplished from Fort Bridger, and the detour through the South Pass and the valley of the Sweetwater, as well as the ruggedness of the Black Hills upon that line, be entirely avoided."

At Fort Bridger, the legendary Jim Bridger again offered to act as Stansbury's guide on yet another trailblazing trip. Bridger's "offer was most cheerfully accepted; and as our route would lay directly through the war-ground of several powerful Indian tribes, care was had fully to equip the party with arms and ammunition necessary for our defense." From the fort, in the southwestern corner of today's Wyoming, the party went eastward across Black's Fork, across the Green River at the head of Flaming Gorge, then along Bitter Creek to a point near Table Rock where "we reached the dividing height between the waters of the Pacific and those of the Atlantic."

From there the party passed near the Medicine Bow River and went on to the Laramie Plains. East of the Laramie River, Stansbury made another significant discovery, Cheyenne Pass, so named from "the constant use made of it by that tribe in their migrations to and from the Platte." Through this pass in the Laramie Mountains a highway and railroad would run in the future, many miles south of the Oregon Trail. (South Pass, initially the major gateway to the West, eventually lost its importance as a passage through the mountains; today no major road traverses what is identified only by a National Historic Landmark.)

Stansbury next headed northward to the "picturesque valley of the Chugwater," and here his explorations came to an end. He "sustained a severe injury from a fall, which not only incapacitated me from mounting my horse, but confined me altogether to my bed until our arrival at Fort Laramie [on Oct. 12, 1850]. It was a source of much satisfaction, under this severe disappointment, that the great object with which we had left Fort Bridger had been successfully attained." He had found a new and shorter route across southern Wyoming, which became today's Interstate Highway 80.

The work of Stansbury and other surveyors who came after culminated at length in the selection of cross-country railroad routes. As Frederick Jackson Turner, historian of the western frontier, noted: "The buffalo trail became the Indian trail, and this became the trader's 'trace'; the trails widened into roads and the roads into turnpikes and these in turn were transformed into railroads."

And the railroads brought even more settlement to the West, turning the potential of "manifest destiny" into the reality of a nation stretching from the Atlantic to the Pacific.

In the introduction to his Report upon the Colorado River of the West, *which was published as a Senate Executive Document, Ives provided a brief background on the Colorado. (The Ives report, published in 1861 by the Government Printing Office, contains many superb sketches and panoramic views, in black and white and color, by Möllhausen and Egloffstein.)*

Chapter 19

JOSEPH IVES: THE LOWER COLORADO RIVER

Before the coming of the transcontinental railroads, much of the West had been explored and charted. One of the major remaining mysteries, however, was the great river of the Southwest, the Colorado.

In December, 1857, Lieutenant Joseph C. Ives of the Corps of Topographical Engineers, embarked on the lower Colorado to determine how far north of Fort Yuma it was navigable, and to explore the terrain south and east of the Grand Canyon. Ives, a native of New York, had attended Yale, graduated from West Point in 1852, and had assisted Amiel Whipple on an 1853 survey of the 35th parallel. He had the experience and the enthusiasm for his assignment, which he himself had requested.

In addition to its scientific objectives—studies of the geology, botany, and zoology of the region—the expedition had a strategic military objective. Ives was to ascertain whether steamboats could supply the military garrisons springing up, or planned for construction, on or adjacent to the Colorado, and see whether trails could be blazed in the difficult, broken terrain east of the river.

Ives noted in his background study the accounts of trappers "who professed to have seen the [Grand] canyon, and propagated among their prairie companions incredible accounts of the stupendous character of the formation ... caused it to be a matter of interest to have the region explored, and to lay down the positions of the Colorado and its tributaries along the unknown belt of country north of the 35th parallel [roughly the route of today's Interstate 40 from Albuquerque to Flagstaff, and across the Colorado River into California at Needles]. The establishment of new military posts in New Mexico and Utah made it also desirable to ascertain how far the river was navigable, and whether it might not prove an avenue for the economical ... transportation of supplies to the newly occupied stations."

For the Ives exploration an iron steamer, the *Explorer*, was, with difficulty, built, tested, shipped in sections, and assembled for the ascent of the river. The *Explorer* reached Fort Yuma after a two-week voyage from the mouth of the Colorado. Fort Yuma, Ives noted, is "not a place to inspire one with regret at leaving, [owing to] the barrenness of the surrounding region, the intense heat, and its loneliness and isolation."

At Fort Yuma, Ives chose 24 men for the boat party, among them Dr. John Newberry, a geologist, his assistant Heinrich Möllhausen, a naturalist and artist, and A. J. Carroll, the steamboat engineer. An overland pack-train, led by Lieutenant Tipton, was instructed to follow along with foodstuffs and supplies that would be needed for the subsequent overland trek. Two Yuma guides were hired to serve as interpreters. Carroll thought the Colorado to be "the queerest river to run a steamboat upon that he has ever met with in his experience as an engineer."

Nonetheless, the *Explorer* steamed past the site of today's Imperial Dam, and past today's Blythe, California, and the valley north of Blythe.

Beyond the Bill Williams River (near the site of Parker Dam, south of Lake Havasu) the *Explorer* entered the Mojave Range, where "a cluster of slender and prominent pinnacles, named by Lieutenant Whipple 'The Needles,' is in close proximity to the river. Mr. Möllhausen enlisted the services of the [Chemehuevi] children to procure zoological specimens, and has obtained, at the cost of a few strings of beads, several varieties of pouched mice and lizards. They think he eats them, and are delighted that his eccentric appetite can be gratified with so much ease and profit to themselves."

The Mojave Canyon was "a scene of such imposing grandeur as I have never before witnessed. As the river wound through the narrow enclosures every turn developed some sublime effect or startling novelty in the view. Brilliant tints of purple, green, brown, red, and white illuminated the stupendous surfaces and relieved their sombre monotony. Far above, distinct upon the narrow strips of sky, turrets, spires, jagged statue-like peaks and grotesque pinnacles overlooked the deep abyss."

The Mojave Indians, Ives wrote: "... regard the steamboat with a ludicrous mixture of amusement, admiration, and distrust. The stern wheel particularly excites remark. It is painted red, their favorite color ..."

The *Explorer* headed for the bend of the Colorado (east of Las Vegas). Beyond Pyramid Canyon (and the site of Davis Dam) the steamboat "entered a region that has never, as far as any records show, been visited by whites, and we are approaching a locality where it is supposed that the famous 'Big Canyon' of the Colorado commences; every point of view is scanned with eager interest." (The party was in what was to become Lake Mead National Recreation Area, created when Hoover Dam was built.)

Passage became increasingly difficult as the *Explorer* approached Black Canyon. "Twenty miles of distance required five days to accomplish. A dozen or more rapids, of all descriptions,

had to be passed; some were violent and deep, others shallow. At a few the bed of the stream was sandy, but generally it was composed of gravel and pebbles.

"A sudden turn around the base of a conical peak disclosed the southern portal of the Black Canyon directly in front. A rapid, a hundred yards below the mouth of the canyon, created a short detention, and a strong head of steam was put on to make the ascent. After passing the crest the current became slack, the soundings were unusually favorable, and we were shooting swiftly past the entrance, eagerly gazing into the mysterious depths beyond, when the *Explorer*, with a stunning crash, brought up abruptly and instantaneously against a sunken rock. For a second the impression was that the canyon had fallen in."

The boat had been badly damaged, but Carroll knew that it was not irreparable. Three days of work "restored it to its former condition. I thought it would be imprudent, after this experience of sunken rocks, to attempt the passage of the canyon without making a preliminary reconnaissance in the skiff."

Ives and two companions sculled the skiff into the Black Canyon. "We entered its gigantic precincts and commenced to thread the mazes of a canyon far exceeding in vastness any that had been yet traversed. The walls were perpendicular, rising in many places sheer from the water for over a thousand feet. The naked rocks presented, in lieu of the brilliant tints that had illuminated the sides of the lower passes, a uniform sombre hue that added much to the solemn and impressive sublimity of the place. The river was narrow and devious, and each turn disclosed new combinations of colossal and fantastic forms. Rapids were of frequent occurrence, and at every one we were obliged to get out of the skiff and haul it over."

Two more days brought them to the mouth of a stream that Ives presumed to be the Virgin. This was as far as he thought it wise to proceed. "I now determined not to try to ascend the Colorado any further. It appeared that the foot of Black Canyon should be considered the practical head of navigation."

While the *Explorer* was being prepared for the return voyage to Fort Yuma, the long-awaited pack train arrived. Lieutenant Tipton reported that "the trip from Fort Yuma had been a rough one; the trails across the mountain ranges were difficult even for pack-mules to follow. The mules were not in the best condition to commence the land explorations," the next phase of Ives' assignment.

The *Explorer* and the pack-train returned to the Mojave villages, where the chief assigned three of his men to guide Ives "to some point on the Colorado above the Great Bend." The *Explorer* steamed down the river toward Fort Yuma, and Ives, with his augmented party, headed overland toward the Grand Canyon.

The party crossed the Black Mountains on a narrow path "under a burning sun, attended with hazard to the weak and heavily-loaded beasts." Beyond the Grand Wash Cliffs was the territory of the Hualpai Indians, never before seen by white men, and at today's Peach Springs three of them appeared.

Ives persuaded the Hualpais to guide his party to the floor of the Grand Canyon. They "were of great assistance, for the ravines crossed and forked in intricate confusion. The descent was great and the trail blind and circuitous. The place grew wilder and grander … we had penetrated into the domestic retreat of the Hualpai nation.

"Our party being, in all probability, the first company of whites that had ever been seen by them, we had anticipated producing a great effect, and were a little chagrined when [an] old woman, and two or three others of both sexes that were met, went by without taking the slightest notice of us. If pack-trains had been in the habit of passing twenty times a day they could not have manifested a more complete indifference."

After an overnight encampment "a short walk down the bed of Diamond River disclosed the mysterious canyon [which] was unrivalled in grandeur. Mr. Möllhausen has taken a sketch, which gives a better idea of it than any description.

"Dr. Newberry had opportunities for observation seldom afforded to the geologist. This plateau formation has been undisturbed by volcanic action, and the sides of the canyons exhibit all of the series that compose the tablelands of New Mexico, presenting, perhaps, the most splendid exposure of stratified rocks that there is in the world."

After examining the floor of the western portion of the Grand Canyon, they tried to obtain information from a small group of Hualpais as to the best way to ascend to the plateau. Led by one of the Mojave guides, the party climbed out to the Coconino Plateau, nearly seven thousand feet above. "A still higher plateau rises to the north. The Colorado is not far distant, and we must be opposite to the most stupendous part of the 'Big Canyon.' The bluffs are in view, but the intervening country is cut up by side canyons and cross ravines, and no place has yet been seen that presents a favorable approach to this gigantic chasm."

Ives could see "further south, eighty miles distant, that vast pile of the San Francisco Mountains [north of Flagstaff], its conical summit covered with snow, and sharply defined against the sky."

The party next followed a trail down to Cataract Canyon, the trail becoming narrower and narrower until, "glancing down the side of my mule I found that he was walking within three inches of the brink of a sheer gulf a thousand feet deep; on the other side, nearly touching my knee, was an almost vertical wall rising to an enormous altitude. The sight made my head swim, and I dismounted and got ahead of the mule, a difficult and delicate operation, which I was thankful to have safely performed. A part of the men became so giddy that they were obliged to creep upon their hands and knees, being unable to walk or stand.

"We were deeper in the bowels of the earth than we had ever been before, and surrounded by walls and towers of such imposing dimensions that it would be useless to attempt describing them." This was the home of the Yampai Indians. "The extent and magnitude of the system of canyons is astounding. The plateau is cut into shreds by these gigantic chasms, and resembles a vast ruin. Belts of country miles in width have been swept away, leaving only isolated mountains standing in the gap. Fissures so profound that the eye cannot penetrate their depths are separated by walls whose thickness one can almost span, and slender spires that seem tottering upon their bases shoot up thousands of feet from the vaults below." The region is, of course, altogether valueless; it can be approached only from the south, and after entering it there is nothing to do but leave. Ours has been the first, and will doubtless be the last, party of whites to visit this profitless locality. It seems intended by nature that the Colorado river, along the greater portion of its lonely and majestic way, shall be forever unvisited and undisturbed."

On the way to the northern base of Bill Williams Mountain, Ives commented: "To eyes that have been resting upon the deserted and ghastly region northward this country appears like a paradise. The melting snows have covered it with green meadows and spring flowers." The exhausting journey through "difficult country and rocky surface" had taken a heavy toll on the mules, which, Ives noted, "look and move like slightly animated skeletons." He now dispatched Lt. Tipton to lead the pack-train to Zuni "while Dr. Newberry, Mr. Egloffstein, and myself, with ten men and a few of the least exhausted mules, are to proceed, to visit the towns of the Moquis [Hopis]" (on the north rim, in Utah, of today's Navajo nation's magnificent, naturally sculpted Monument Valley, which extends southward into Arizona).

They followed an Indian trail to the Little Colorado River (called the Flax River by Ives), and then went northward through a section of desert (the Painted Desert) "where scorpions, spiders, rattlesnakes, and centipedes emerged from their retreats to enjoy the evening air."

Two Hopi Indians met the party and offered to serve as guides to Mooshahneh (Mishongnovi) pueblo. From atop the mesa "we beheld a magnificent panorama. The San Francisco mountain, the valley and canyon of Flax River, and the plateaus to the north and east were all visible. Several trails radiated from the foot of the bluff in perfectly straight lines, and could be traced a long way over the level surface. One conducted to the canyon of Flax river; another was the trail of the Apaches; another that of the Coyoteros, a fourth came from Zuni, and still further east was the Navajo trail leading to Fort Defiance.

"From these heights, the ascent to which is so difficult and so easily defended, the Moquis can overlook the surrounding country and decry, at a vast distance, the approach of strangers. The towns themselves would be almost impregnable to an Indian assault. Each pueblo is built around a rectangular court. The exterior walls, which are of stone, have no openings, and would have to be scaled or battered down before access could be gained to the interior."

The Ives party was guided to Oraibi, Ives describing the friendly Hopis as being, "all . . . wrapped in Navajo blankets, with broad white and dark stripes, and a crowd at a distance looks like the face of a stratified rock."

From Oraibi, in the company of a group of Hopis, Ives marched to Fort Defiance, a military post near today's Window Rock, where on May 23, 1858, the exploration came to an end.

Soon after Ives' declaration that the Colorado was navigable as far as Black Canyon, traffic on the river was begun. Steamers were utilized at first to transport military supplies and troops, and later to serve the mining sites that were springing up on and near the river. The traffic survived for some fifty years until the waters of the river were diverted to irrigate the Imperial Valley—and to create the Salton Sea—and were obstructed by the erection of dams and power plants.

Although Ives did not foresee the future of the glorious wilderness of northern Arizona—"Most of it is uninhabitable, and a great deal of it is impassable"—an enlightened nation later did. Nor did Ives foresee that his journals and Newberry's scientific studies would be useful to a man who would dare, ten years later, to explore what Ives believed to be an impenetrable section of the Colorado River—its Grand Canyon.

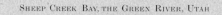
SHEEP CREEK BAY, THE GREEN RIVER, UTAH

This historic journey is chronicled in Powell's masterpiece of Western adventure, Exploration of the Colorado River of the West and Its Tributaries.

Chapter 20

JOHN WESLEY POWELL: THE EXPLORATION OF THE GRAND CANYON

The last of the great explorations in the American West produced the last of the great chronicles, a narrative of the descent of the Green River into the Colorado River and through the awe-inspiring Grand Canyon to the mouth of the Virgin River, by a party under the command of the intrepid, one-armed John Wesley Powell.

Born in upstate New York in 1834, Powell was a schoolteacher who had lived in Ohio and Illinois. He had fought in the Civil War, and at the Battle of Shiloh suffered the loss of his right arm below the elbow. Despite this disability he remained in active service, attaining the rank of major. After the war he became a professor at Illinois Wesleyan College, established a natural history museum at Bloomington, and led expeditions to the Rockies to collect fauna and flora.

During his mountain trips Powell developed an intense curiosity about the unknown areas of the Colorado River, especially its mysterious and majestic Grand Canyon, and determined to become the first to explore there. On his own he raised money, commissioned the building of four specially designed boats, and recruited and trained ten men. With a few members of his party he prepared for the Colorado exploration by spending the summer of 1867 and the winter of 1868-69 reconnoitering the tributary streams and the canyons of the Green and Grand rivers.

The Colorado River, whose upper stream was known in Powell's time as the Grand River, rises in the Rockies near Long's Peak in Colorado. It descends to a confluence with the Green River north of Cataract Canyon in Utah, and flows through southern Utah's Glen Canyon National Recreation Area into Arizona, just above Page. There it makes its way through Marble Canyon and bends westward to roar through Grand Canyon. Beyond the Virgin River and Lake Mead it bends southward to form Arizona's border with the southern tip of Nevada, just east of Lake Mead National Recreation Area. From above Needles, it flows along the border between Arizona and California, past Yuma, and finally enters the Gulf of California in northern Mexico.

The long stretch of the Colorado River from the Green to the Virgin had never been explored or navigated. The Green itself, which at the time of Powell's exploration was regarded as the upper stream of the Colorado, had been navigated by William Ashley in 1825, but only as far south as the Duchesne River.

On May 24, 1869, John Powell and his companions set off on a historic journey from Green River City in Wyoming "to descend the Green to the Colorado, and the Colorado down to the foot of the Grand Canyon ... The good people of Green River City turned out to see us start."

Past the mouth of Black's Fork and Henry's Fork, the Green River "enters the [Uinta Mountain] range by a flaring, red gorge. This is the first of the canyons we are about to explore—an introductory one to a series made by the river through this range. We name it Flaming Gorge."

FLAMING GORGE

GREEN RIVER IN UTAH

Looking toward the confluence of the Green and Colorado Rivers in Canyonlands National Park

Powell and a party "go to the summit of the cliff on the left." He and George Y. Bradley, also a Civil War veteran, "climb more than a thousand feet to a point where we can see the stream sweeping in a long, beautiful curve through the gorge below."

"Looking to the west we can see the valley of Henry's Fork though which, for many miles, the little river flows in a tortuous channel. For many years this valley has been the home of a number of mountaineers, who were originally hunters and trappers, living with the Indians."

It was the morning when the party was "ready to enter the mysterious canyon [Flaming Gorge] . . . Soon our boats reach the swift current; a stroke or two, now on this side, now on that, and we thread the narrow passage with exhilarating velocity, mounting the high waves, whose foaming crests dash over us, and plunging into the troughs until we reach the quiet water below. Then comes a feeling of great relief. Our first rapid is run."

After running through, and naming, Horseshoe Canyon, Kingfisher Canyon, and Beehive Point, Powell came to another set of rapids, which he regarded as too dangerous to attempt. "We run our boats down with lines." Then "we have an exciting ride. The river rolls down the canyon at a wonderful rate, and with no rocks in the way we make almost railroad speed."

The boats are now in calm water but "a threatening roar is heard in the distance. Slowly approaching the point whence the sound issues, we come next to falls, and tie up just above them. Here we shall be compelled to make a portage. We make a trail among the rocks, transport the cargoes to a point below the falls, let the boats over, and are ready to start before noon.

Dinosaur National Monument

"On a high rock by which the trail passes we find the inscription: 'Ashley 18-5.' The third figure is obscure—some of the party reading it 1835, some 1855. [The date was 1825. Powell was unfamiliar with this historic first descent of the Green since Ashley's journals had not yet been published.] Ashley Falls is the name we give to the cataract."

Next came Red Canyon and then Swallow Canyon in Brown's Park. Powell climbed a rise and "to the east we look up the valley of the Vermilion, through which Frémont found his path on his way to the great parks of Colorado."

After a night in Brown's Park: "I am wakened by a chorus of birds. It seems as if all the feathered songsters of the region have come to the old tree. Several species of warblers, woodpeckers, and flickers above, meadow larks in the grass, and wild geese in the river. I recline on my elbow and watch a lark near by, and then awaken my bedfellow to listen to my Jenny Lind. A real morning concert for me; none of your 'matinees'!"

They traveled into what they named the Canyon of Lodore, where the party lost a boat, but rescued the men in it. They named it Disaster Falls.

At the mouth of the Yampa River (in the Colorado section of today's Dinosaur National Monument just east of the Utah state line) Powell had a harrowing experience. He and Bradley were climbing what Powell called Echo Rock, and as they approached the summit of the cliff Powell found himself in a crevice from which he could "get no farther and cannot step back." The near tragedy was avoided when Bradley climbed above him, took off his drawers and swung them down for Powell to grasp.

On June 28, having been on the river for more than a month, the party came to the mouth of the Duchesne River, up which the men tried to row "but we are not able to make much headway against the swift current, and hence conclude we must walk all the way to the agency [reservation of the Uinta Indians]."

After a week's sojourn at the Indian agency on the Ute reservation, the party was back on Green River. Below the Duchesne River was "a region of the wildest desolation. The canyon is very tortuous, the river very rapid, and many lateral canyons enter on either side. We are minded to call this the Canyon of Desolation."

With great trouble the Powell party ran the rapids of Desolation Canyon and proceeded through Gray Canyon, where they discovered an Indian crossing.

Beyond the San Rafael River, "there is an exquisite charm in our ride today down this beautiful [Labyrinth] canyon. It gradually grows deeper with every mile of travel; the walls are symmetrically curved and grandly arched, of a beautiful color, and reflected in the quiet waters in many places so as almost to deceive the eye and suggest to the beholder the thought that he is looking into profound depths. We are all in fine spirits and feel very gay. Now and then we whistle or shout or discharge a pistol, to listen to the reverberations among the cliffs."

In Stillwater Canyon "the stream is still quiet, and we glide along through a strange, weird, grand region. The landscape everywhere, away from the river, is rock, crags of rock, ten thousand strangely carved forms; rocks everywhere, and no vegetation, no soil, no sand. In long gentle curves the river winds about these rocks.

"When thinking of these rocks one must not conceive of piles of boulders or heaps of fragments, but of a whole land of naked rock, with giant forms carved on it; cathedral-shaped buttes, towering hundreds or thousands of feet, cliffs that cannot be scaled, and canyon walls that shrink the river into insignificance, with vast, hollow domes and tall pinnacles and shafts set on the verge overhead; and all highly colored—buff, gray, red, brown, and chocolate —never lichened, never moss-covered, but bare, and often polished."

On July 18, almost two months after embarkation, the party came to the confluence of the Green and the Grand rivers, and was on the banks of the Colorado.

VIEW FROM SOUTH KAIBAB TRAIL

Powell climbed a bordering cliff: "What a world of grandeur is spread before us! Below is the canyon through which the Colorado runs. We can trace its course for miles, and at points catch glimpses of the river. From the northwest comes the Green in a narrow winding gorge. From the northeast comes the Grand through a canyon that seems bottomless from where we stand."

"July 21—We start this morning on the Colorado. The river is rough, and bad rapids in close succession are found."

The next day "we come at once to difficult rapids and falls that in many places are more abrupt than in any of the canyons through which we have passed, and we decide to name this Cataract Canyon."

GOOSE NECK POINT

SOUTH KAIBAB TRAIL

Beyond Cataract Canyon, a difficult voyage of 41 miles, the party came to the "mouth of a stream which enters from the right. Into this our little boat is turned. The water is exceedingly muddy and has an unpleasant odor. One of the men in the boat following shouts to Dunn [a hunter from Colorado] and asks whether it is a trout stream. Dunn replies, much disgusted, that it is 'a dirty devil,' and by this name the river is to be known hereafter."

The Dirty Devil is where Powell discovered ancient ruins atop a cliff, and on the face of the cliff many etchings. He was in an area of ruins extending for some fifteen miles along the river. While attempting to examine them he was "surprised at finding a stairway, evidently cut in the rock by hands. At one place where there is a vertical wall of 10 or 12 feet, I find an old rickety ladder. It may be that this was a watchtower of the ancient people whose homes we have found in ruins."

Coming through the long canyon beyond Dirty Devil River "we discover the mouth of the San Juan." At an evening encampment in a "vast chamber carved out of the rock," Powell's brother "sings us a song at night; we are pleased to find that this hollow in the rock is filled with sweet sounds. It was doubtless made for an academy of music by its storm-born architect; so we name it Music Temple."

In the canyon they were enchanted by "a curious ensemble of wonderful features—carved walls, royal arches, glens, alcove gulches, mounds, and monuments. From which of these features shall we select a name? We decide to call it Glen Canyon."

Descending Glen Canyon "we glide hour after hour, stopping now and then, as our attention is arrested by some new wonder, until we reach a point which is historic. In the year 1776, Father Escalante, a Spanish priest, made an expedition from Santa Fe to the northwest, crossing the Grand and Green, and then passing down the Wasatch Mountains and the southern plateaus until he reached the Rio Virgen. His intention was to cross to the Mission of Monterey; but, from information he received from the Indians, he decided that the route was impracticable. Not wishing to return to Santa Fe over the circuitous route by which he had just traveled, he attempted to go by one more direct, which led him across the Colorado at a point known as El Vado de Los Padres [the Crossing of the Fathers]."

At the end of the long run through Glen Canyon, "the whole character of the canyon changed" as Powell came to the site of the Lee's Ferry Marina. "Here the canyon terminates abruptly in a line of cliffs, which stretches from either side across the river."

VIEW FROM NANKOWEAP

RAINBOW BRIDGE AT GLEN CANYON

The next canyon entered by the party was so awesome it filled the men with anxiety, but so beautiful that Powell named it Marble Canyon. "The limestone of this canyon is often polished, and makes a beautiful marble. Sometimes the rocks are of many colors—white, gray, pink, and purple, with saffron tints. It is with very great labor that we make progress, meeting with many obstructions, running rapids, letting down our boats with lines from rock to rock, and sometimes carrying boats and cargoes around bad places. At one place I have a walk for more than a mile on a marble pavement, all polished and fretted with strange devices and embossed in a thousand fantastic patterns."

Marble Canyon

The party made camp below the Little Colorado and on August 13, "we are now ready to start on our way down the Great Unknown. We have but a month's ration remaining. The sugar has melted and gone on its way down the river." Most of the flour has been drenched and spoiled. Most of the bacon has turned rotten. A few pounds of dried apples are still edible.

"We are three-quarters of a mile in the depths of the earth, and the great river shrinks into insignificance as it dashes its angry waves against the walls and cliffs that rise to the world above. We have an unknown distance yet to run, an unknown river to explore. What falls there are we know not; what rocks beset the channel, we know not; what walls rise over the river, we know not. Ah well! we may conjecture many things. The men talk as cheerfully as ever; jests are bandied about freely this morning, but to me the cheer is somber and the jests are ghastly."

The first day's run in the Grand Canyon went well, but on the second day the boats entered a granite gorge. "At the very introduction it inspires awe. The canyon is narrower than we have ever before seen; the water is swifter; there are but few broken rocks in the channel, but the walls are set on either side with pinnacles and crags; and sharp angular buttresses, bristling with wind- and wave-polished spires, extend far out into the river.

"We hear a great roar ahead, and approach it very cautiously. The sound grows louder and louder as we run, and at last we find ourselves above a long, broken fall, with ledges and pinnacles of rock obstructing the river. There is a descent of perhaps 75 or 80 feet in a third of a mile, and the rushing waters break into great waves on the rocks, and lash themselves into a mad, white foam.

"We can land just above, but there is no foothold on either side by which we can make a portage. It is nearly a thousand feet to the top of the granite; we must run the rapid or abandon the river.

"There is no hesitation. We step into our boats, push off, and away we go, first on smooth but swift water, then we strike a glassy wave and ride to its top, down again into the trough, up again on a higher wave, and down and up on waves higher and still higher until we strike one just as it curls back, and a breaker rolls over our little boat. Still on we speed, shooting past projecting rocks, till the little boat is caught in a whirlpool and spun round several times."

When the rapids were too turbulent, and the riverbanks permitted, the men came ashore to let the boats down by lines. "It is not easy to describe the labor of such navigation. We must prevent the waves from dashing the boats against the cliffs. Where we wish to run her out a little way from shore through a channel between the rocks, we first throw in little sticks of driftwood and watch their course, to see where we must steer so that she will pass the channel in safety. And so we hold, and let go, and pull, and lift, and ward—among rocks, around rocks, and over rocks."

Once the boats enter smooth water "we discover a stream entering from the north—a clear, beautiful creek, coming down through a gorgeous red canyon. We land and camp on a sand

beach above its mouth, under a great, overspreading tree with willow-shaped leaves." Powell named it Bright Angel Creek.

On August 18, "while the men are at work making portages I climb up the granite to the summit and go away back over the rust-colored sandstones and greenish-yellow shales to the foot of the marble wall. I climb so high that the men and boats are lost in the black depths below and the dashing river is a rippling brook, and there is still more canyon above than below. All about me are interesting geologic records. All about me are grand views, too, for the clouds are playing again in the gorges. But somehow I think of the nine days' rations and the bad river, and the lesson of the rocks and the glory of the scene are but half conceived."

In the "bad river" a day later, Powell's boat overturned. "We are some distance in advance of the larger boats. The river is rough and swift and we are unable to land, but cling to the boat and are carried downstream over another rapid. The men in the boats above see our trouble, but they are caught in whirlpools and are spinning about in eddies, and it seems a long time before they come to our relief. At last they do come; our boat is turned right side up and bailed out."

But there was no respite in the boiling river. "I stand on deck, supporting myself with a strap fastened on either side of the gunwale. The boat glides rapidly where the water is smooth, then, striking a wave, she leaps and bounds like a thing of life, and we have a wild, exhilarating ride. The excitement is so great that we forget the danger until we hear the roar of a great fall below; then we back on our oars, are carried slowly toward its head and succeed in landing just above, and find that we have to make another portage."

Now there were "many rapids, but none so bad that we cannot run them with safety." On a quiet stretch of the river "we discover an Indian garden at the foot of the wall on the right, just where a little stream with a narrow flood plain comes down through a side canyon. Along the valley Indians have planted corn, using for irrigation the water which bursts out in springs at the foot of the cliff." (The Havasupai still dwell in the canyon today.) "The corn is looking quite well, but is not sufficiently advanced to give us roasting ears; but there are some nice green squashes. We carry ten or a dozen of these on board our boats and hurriedly leave, not willing to be caught in the robbery, yet excusing ourselves by pleading our great want. We run down a short distance to where we feel certain no Indian can follow, and what a kettle of squash sauce we make!"

Powell clambers "up over the granite pinnacles for a mile or two" to reconnoiter what lies ahead, can see no way to portage around what appears to be the most dangerous stretch of river they have yet come to, and fears that "to run it would be sure destruction. In my eagerness to reach a point where I can see the roaring fall below, I go too far on the wall, and can neither advance or retreat. [Again!] I stand with one foot on a little projecting rock and cling with my hand fixed in a little crevise. Finding I am caught here, suspended 400 feet above the river, into which I must fall if my footing fails, I call for help."

After another dramatic rescue, Powell decided that the boats must try to run the rapids and falls ahead. He determined that "we must be about 45 miles from the Rio Virgen. If we can reach that point, we know that there are settlements up that river about 20 miles. This 45 miles in a direct line will probably be 80 or 90 by the meandering line of the river. But then we know that there is comparatively open country for many miles above the mouth of the Virgen, which is our point of destination."

All night long Powell paced "up and down a little path, on a few yards of sand beach, along by the river. Is it wise to go on? I almost conclude to leave the river. But for years I have been contemplating this trip. To leave the exploration unfinished, to say there is a part of the canyon which I cannot explore, having already nearly accomplished it, is more than I am willing to acknowledge, and I determine to go on."

The incredible journey was almost at an end. After two more narrow escapes from disaster, Powell and his men had conquered the river and emerged "from the Grand Canyon of the Colorado. The relief from danger and the joy of success are great. Every waking hour passed in the Grand Canyon has been one of toil. We have watched with deep solicitude the steady disappearance of our scant supply of rations, and from time to time have seen the river snatch a portion of the little left, while we were a-hungered. And danger and toil were endured in those gloomy depths, where oftimes clouds hid the sky by day and but a narrow zone of stars could be seen at night. Only during the few hours of deep sleep, consequent on hard labor, has the roar of the waters been hushed.

"Now the danger is over, now the toil has ceased, now the gloom has disappeared, now the firmament is bounded only by the horizon, and what a vast expanse of constellations can be seen! The river rolls by us in silent majesty; the quiet of the camp is sweet; our joy is almost ecstasy. We sit till long after midnight talking of the Grand Canyon, talking of home . . ."

The party proceeded to the mouth of the Virgin River where they met three Mormons and an Indian who "seem far less surprised to see us than we do to see them. They evidently know who we are, and on talking with them they tell us that we have been reported lost long ago, and that some weeks before a messenger had been sent from Salt Lake City with instructions for them to watch for any fragments or relics of our party that might drift down the stream."

John Wesley Powell and his men—Sumner, Bradley, Hawkins, Hall, and Walter Powell—had completed the last great epic exploration in the American West. In descending the Green, and conquering the Colorado in their vulnerable boats, they had achieved the improbable, if not the impossible. Only those who have since made the thrilling river descent can fully appreciate Powell's great and unique accomplishment.

A year later, in 1870, Powell returned to the West, "determined to resume the exploration of the canyons of the Colorado." His description of the Grand Canyon is as true today as it was in 1869: "It is the land of music. The river thunders in perpetual roar, swelling in floods of music when the storm gods play the rocks, and fading away in soft and low murmurs when the infinite blue of heaven is unveiled. With the melody of the great tide rising and falling, swelling and vanishing forever, other melodies are heard in the gorges of the lateral canyons, while the waters plunge in the rapids among the rocks or leap in great cataracts.

COLORADO RIVER

"Thus the Grand Canyon is a land of song. Mountains of music swell in the rivers, hills of music billow in the creeks, and meadows of music murmur in the rills that ripple over the rocks. Altogether it is a symphony of multitudinous melodies. All this is the music of waters. The glories and the beauties of form, color, and sound unite in the Grand Canyon—forms unrivaled even by the mountains, colors that vie with sunsets, and sounds that span the diapason from tempest to tinkling raindrop, from cataract to bubbling fountain."

With Powell's magnificent achievement, the monumental task of exploring the wilderness of the West had come to an end. Without the journals and memoirs written by the pathfinders, travelers, and explorers of the West, its history and opening would today be as unknown as the *terra incognita* which they explored.

VULCAN'S ANVIL AT MILE 178

REFERENCES

American Heritage. *Natural Wonders of America.* New York: American Heritage Publishing Co., 1972.

Bartlett, John R. *Personal Narrative of Explorations and Incidents.* 2 vols. Chicago: The Rio Grande Press, 1965.

Bell, James Christy, Jr. *Opening a Highway to the Pacific 1838-1846.* New York: AMS Press, 1968 (reprinted with the permission of Columbia University Press).

Billington, Ray Allen. *America's Frontier Heritage.* New York: Holt, Rinehart and Winston, 1963.

———. *The Far Western Frontier 1830-1860.* New York: Harper & Row, 1956.

Bonner, T. D. *The Life and Adventures of James P. Beckwourth.* Edited by Bernard DeVoto. New York: Alfred A. Knopf, 1931.

Burroughs, Raymond D., ed. *The Natural History of the Lewis and Clark Expedition.* Ann Arbor: The Michigan State University Press, 1961.

Catlin, George. *Letters & Notes on the North American Indians.* Edited by Michael Mooney. New York: Clarkson N. Potter, 1975.

Chittenden, Hiram Martin. *The American Fur Trade of the Far West.* 3 vols. New York: Francis P. Harper, 1902.

Cleland, Robert Glass. *This Reckless Breed of Men: The Trappers and Fur Traders of the Southwest.* New York: Alfred A. Knopf, 1950.

Cromie, Alice. *Tour Guide to the Old West.* New York: Quadrangle/The New York Times Book Company, 1977.

DeVoto, Bernard. *Across the Wide Missouri.* Boston: Houghton Mifflin Company, 1947.

———. *The Course of Empire.* Boston: Houghton Mifflin Company, 1952.

———. *The Year of Decision 1846.* Boston: Houghton Mifflin Company, 1942.

Douglas, Walter B. *Manuel Lisa.* With additions annotated and edited by Abraham P. Nasatir. New York: Argosy-Antiquarian, Ltd., 1964.

Duffus, Robert L. *The Santa Fe Trail.* New York: David McKay Company, 1975.

Garrard, Lewis H. *Wah-to-yah and the Taos Trail.* Norman: University of Oklahoma Press, 1955.

Ghent, W. J. *The Early Far West.* New York: Tudor Publishing Co., 1936.

Gilbert, E. W. *The Exploration of Western America 1800-1850.* New York: Cooper Square Publishers, Inc., 1966 (reprinted by permission of Cambridge University Press).

Goetzmann, William H. *Exploration and Empire.* New York: W. W. Norton & Company, 1966.

Hafen, LeRoy R. *Broken Hand, The Life of Thomas Fitzpatrick.* Denver: The Old West Publishing Company, 1931.

Haines, Francis D., Jr. *The Snake Country Expedition of 1830-1831: John Work's Field Journal*. Norman: University of Oklahoma Press, 1971.

Hawgood, John A. *America's Western Frontier*. New York: Alfred A. Knopf, 1967.

Klose, Nelson. *A Concise Study Guide to the American Frontier*. Lincoln: University of Nebraska Press, 1964.

Lavender, David. *The Fist in the Wilderness*. Albuquerque: University of New Mexico Press, 1964.

——. *Land of Giants: The Drive to the Pacific Northwest*. Lincoln: University of Nebraska Press, 1979.

——. *Westward Vision: The Story of the Oregon Trail*. London: Eyre & Spottiswoode Ltd., Frontier Library, 1963.

Linton, Calvin D., ed. *The Bicentennial Almanac*. Nashville: Thomas Nelson, Inc., 1975.

McCaleb, Walter F. *The Conquest of the West*. New York: Prentice-Hall, 1947.

McDermott, John F., ed. *Travelers on the Western Frontier*. Urbana: University of Illinois Press, 1970.

Parkman, Francis. *The Journals of Francis Parkman*. Edited by Mason Wade. London: Eyre & Spottiswoode, no date.

——. *The Oregon Trail*. New York: Random House, 1949.

Paxson, Frederic L. *History of the American Frontier*. Boston, Houghton Mifflin Company, 1924.

Ruxton, George F. *Life in the Far West*. Edited by LeRoy Hafen. Norman: University of Oklahoma Press, 1951.

——. *Wild Life in the Rocky Mountains*. New York: The MacMillan Company, 1926.

Shepherd, William R. *Historical Atlas*. New York: Barnes & Noble, Inc., 1964.

Stegner, Wallace. *Mormon Country*. New York: Duell, Sloan & Pearce, 1942.

Stewart, George R. *The California Trail*. New York: McGraw-Hill, 1962.

Trager, James. *The People's Chronology*. New York: Holt, Rinehart and Winston, 1979.

Turner, Henry S. *The Original Journals of Henry Smith Turner, with Stephen Watts Kearny to New Mexico and California 1846-1847*. Edited by Dwight L. Clarke. Norman: University of Oklahoma Press, 1966.

Vandiveer, Clarence A. *The Fur-Trade and Early Western Exploration*. New York: Cooper Square Publishers, 1971.

Young, Otis. *The First Military Escort on the Santa Fe Trail 1829*. Glendale, Calif.: The Arthur H. Clark Company, 1952.

The Black Canyon of the Gunnison in Colorado

PRIMARY SOURCES

Abert, Lt. James W. *Report of J. W. Abert on his Examination of New Mexico in the Years 1846-1847*. 30th Cong., 1st sess., 1848. House Exec. Doc. 31.

Becknell, William. *Journal of Two Expeditions from Boon's Lick to Santa Fe*. Missouri Historical Society Collections, vol. 2, 1906.

Bell, John R. *Journal of the S. H. Long Expedition; in Far West and Rockies Series*, vol. VI. Glendale, Calif.: Arthur H. Clark Company, 1957.

Bidwell, John. *Echoes of the Past About California*. Edited by Milo M. Quaife. Chicago: The Lakeside Press, 1928.

Brackenridge, H. M. "The Journal of a Voyage up the Missouri River in 1811." Reprinted in *Early Western Travels, vol. 6*. Edited by Reuben Gold Thwaites. Cleveland: Arthur H. Clark Company, 1905.

Bradbury, John. *Travels in the Interior of America*. Printed for the author. London: Sherwood, Neely, and Jones, 1817. Readex Micro-Print, 1966.

Chittenden, H. M., and A. T. Richardson. *Life, Letters and Travels of Father Pierre-Jean De Smet, S. J.* New York: Francis P. Harper, 1905.

Clyman, James. *American Frontiersman*. Edited by Charles L. Camp. San Francisco: California Historical Society, 1928.

Cox, Ross. *Adventures on the Columbia River*. New York: J. & J. Harper, 1832.

Dale, Harrison C. *The Ashley-Smith Explorations and the Discovery of a Central Route to the Pacific 1822-1829, with the original journals*. Cleveland: Arthur H. Clark Company, 1918.

Dawson, Nicholas. *Biography*. San Francisco: The Grabhorn Press, 1933.

Emory, Lt. William H. *Notes of a Military Reconnaissance from Fort Leavenworth, in Missouri, to San Diego in California, 1846-1847*. 30th Cong., 1st sess., 1848. Senate Exec. Doc. 7.

Farnham, Thomas J. *Travels in the Great Western Prairies*. New York: published by the author, 1843.

Ferris, Warren A. *Life in the Rocky Mountains 1830-1835*. Salt Lake City: Rocky Mountain Book Shop, 1940.

Flores, Dan L. *Jefferson & Southwestern Exploration: The Freeman & Custis Accounts of the Red River Expedition of 1806*. Norman: University of Oklahoma Press, 1984.

Fowler, Jacob. *The Journal of Jacob Fowler*. Edited by Elliott Coues. New York: Francis P. Harper, 1898.

Franchere, Gabriel. *Narrative of a Voyage to the Northwest Coast of America*. Translated and edited by J. V. Huntington. New York: Redfield, 1854. Reprint. Chicago: The Lakeside Press, 1954.

Frémont, John C. *The Expeditions of John Charles Frémont.* Edited by Donald Jackson and Mary Lee Spence. Urbana: University of Illinois Press, 1970.

——. *His Narrative of Explorations and Adventures.* New York: Miller, Orton & Mulligan, 1856.

Gregg, Josiah. *The Commerce of the Prairies*. Edited by Milo M. Quaife. Chicago: The Lakeside Press, 1926.

Hastings, Lanford. *The Emigrants' Guide to Oregon and California*. New York: DaCapo Press, 1969.

Irving, Washington. *Astoria, or Anecdotes of an Enterprise Beyond the Rocky Mountains.* Philadelphia: Carey, Lea and Blanchard, 1836.

——. *The Rocky Mountains: or, Scenes, Incidents and Adventures in the Far West, digested from the Journal of Captain B. L. E. Bonneville.* Philadelphia: Carey, Lea and Blanchard, 1837.

Ives, Lt. Joseph C. *Report upon the Colorado River of the West.* 36th Cong., 1st sess., 1861. Senate Exec. Doc. 90.

James, Edwin. "Account of an Expedition from Pittsburgh to the Rocky Mountains." Reprinted in *Early Western Travels, vols. 14-18.* Edited by Reuben Gold Thwaites. Cleveland: Arthur H. Clark Company, 1895.

James, Thomas. *Three Years Among the Indians and Mexicans.* Waterloo, Ill.: published by the author, 1846. Reprint. Chicago: The Lakeside Press.

Kendall, George W. *Narration of the Texan Santa Fe Expedition*. New York: Harper and Brothers, 1844.

Leonard, Zenas. *Narrative of the Adventures of Zenas Leonard.* Edited by Milo M. Quaife. Chicago: The Lakeside Press, 1934.

Lewis, Meriwether, and William Clark. *History of the Expedition under the Command of Lewis and Clark*. Edited by Elliott Coues. New York: Francis P. Harper, 1893.

——. *The Journals of Lewis and Clark*. Edited by Bernard DeVoto. Boston: Houghton Mifflin Company, 1953.

——. *The Original Journals of Lewis and Clark*. Edited by Reuben Gold Thwaites. New York: Dodd, Mead & Company, 1904-5.

Marcy, Capt. Randolph. *Exploration of the Red River of Louisiana, in the year 1852*. 32nd Cong., 2nd sess., 1852. Senate Exec. Doc. 52.

McDermott, John F. *The Western Journals of Dr. George Hunter*. Philadelphia: The American Philosophical Society, 1963.

Nichols, Roger L. *The Missouri Expedition 1818-1820: The Journal of Surgeon John Gale*. Norman: University of Oklahoma Press, 1969.

Nuttall, Thomas. *Journal of Travel into the Arkansas Territory 1819*. Philadelphia: Thos. M. Palmer, 1821. Reprinted in *Early Western Travels, vol. 13*. Edited by Reuben Gold Thwaites. Cleveland: Arthur H. Clark Company.

Parker, Samuel. *Journal of an Exploring Tour Beyond the Rocky Mountains*. Ithaca, N.Y.: published by the author, 1838.

Pike, Zebulon Montgomery. *An Account of Expeditions to the Sources of the Mississippi, and through the Western Parts of Louisiana* … Philadelphia: C.& A. Conrad & Company, 1810.

——. *The Journals of Zebulon Montgomery Pike*. Edited by Donald Jackson. Norman: University of Oklahoma Press, 1966.

——. *The Southwestern Expedition of Zebulon M. Pike*. Edited by Milo M. Quaife. Chicago: The Lakeside Press, 1925.

Powell, John Wesley. *Exploration of the Colorado River of the West and its Tributaries*. Washington, D.C., U.S. Government Printing Office, 1875.

Rollins, Philip A., ed. *The Discovery of the Oregon Trail: Robert Stuart's Narratives* … New York: Charles Scribner's Sons, 1935.

Ross, Alexander. *Adventures of the First Settlers on the Oregon or Columbia River, 1810-1813*. Reprinted in *Early Western Travels, vol. 7*. Edited by Reuben Gold Thwaites. Cleveland: Arthur H. Clark Company, 1904.

Rowland, Mrs. Dunbar. *Life, Letters and Papers of William Dunbar* (incl. *Journal of a Voyage*). Jackson: Press of the Mississippi Historical Society, 1930.

Simpson, Lt. James H. *Journal of a Military Reconnaissance from Santa Fe, New Mexico, to the Navajo Country.* 31st Cong., 1st sess., 1850. Senate Exec. Doc. 64.

Sitgreaves, Capt. Lorenzo. *Report of an Expedition Down the Zuni and Colorado Rivers.* 33rd Cong., 2nd sess., 1853. Senate Exec. Doc. 59.

Stansbury, Capt. Howard. *Exploration and Survey of the Valley of the Great Salt Lake of Utah.* 32nd Cong, spec. sess., 1852. Senate Exec. Doc. 3.

Sullivan, Maurice S. *The Travels of Jedediah Smith ... Including the Journal of the Great American Pathfinder.* Santa Ana, California: The Fine Arts Press, 1934.

Todd, Edgeley, ed. *The Adventures of Captain Bonneville.* Norman: University of Oklahoma Press, 1961.

Townsend, John Kirk. *Narrative of a Journey across the Rocky Mountains to the Columbia River.* Lincoln: University of Nebraska Press, 1978.

Whipple, Lt. Amiel W. *Report of Explorations for a Railway Route near the Thirty-Fifth Parallel of North Latitude from the Mississippi River to the Pacific Ocean.* Pacific Survey Reports. 33rd Cong., 2nd sess., 1853. Senate Exec. Doc. 78.

Wilkes, Lt. Charles. *Narrative of the United States Exploring Expedition 1838-1842.* Philadelphia: Lea and Blanchard, 1845.

Wyeth, John. *Oregon.* Cambridge, Mass.: published by the author, 1833. Readex Micro-Print, 1966.

Wyeth, Nathaniel. *The Correspondence and Journals of Captain Nathaniel J. Wyeth 1831-6.* Edited by F .G. Young. Oregon Historical Society, Eugene: University Press, 1899.

A note on the author

Gerald Roscoe graduated from Harvard and for some years was a feature writer and book reviewer for the *Boston Globe*. He wrote and produced syndicated radio programs and was an advertising executive in New York. Mr. Roscoe was for many years an ardent student of the Trans-Mississippi West, its history, literature, geography, and topography. The present text is drawn from a much longer and more comprehensive work, as witness the Sources and References. Mr. Roscoe died in April 1995, shortly before the manuscript was set in type.

Since 1985, Mr. Roscoe had resided in Thailand where the following books written by him have been published: *The Good Life: A Guide to Buddhism for the Westerner; The Monastic Life: The Pathway of the Buddhist Monk; The Buddha's Life: Man and Myth, Fact and Fable; and The Triple Gem: An Introduction to Buddhism.*

THE PLAINS OF THE HUMBOLDT RIVER

LOOKING TOWARD THE GREAT SAND DUNES NATIONAL MONUMENT